Johnston & Gill

UNDERGROUND
PROPORTIONS OF STANDARD
— BULLSEYE DESIGN. —

NOTE.

100 units on this drawing are equal
to   on drawing Nº
being actually an enlargement of
      times, the design shown hereon.

Standard "Underground" lettering.
copy of alphabet on application.
Large 'U' & 'D' 19 units high. 2½ thick
remaining letters 10 units high. 1½"

33 units radius

WHITE

100 units

24 units

135 units

WHITE

White legend on
dark blue ground.

½ unit white
1 " black
15 units bright red
½ unit black

ed design Nº 659,824 (if flat).
   "   Nº 659,822 (if any part in relief).

OFFICE OF THE SIGNAL ENGINEER
(Chief Engineer's Dept.)

Drg No. B.L.1372

JOHNSTON & GILL

Very British Types

Mark Ovenden

LUND HUMPHRIES

First published in 2016 by Lund Humphries

Lund Humphries

Office 3, Book House

261A City Road

London

EC1V 1JX

UK

www.lundhumphries.com

© Mark Ovenden, 2016

ISBN: 978-1-84822-176-5

A Cataloguing-in-Publication record for this book is available
from the British Library

Copy edited by Kate Parker
Designed by Crow Books
Set in Johnston100 (with thanks to TfL) and Gill Sans Nova
(with thanks to Monotype)
Printed in Slovakia

Frontispiece

The cover for the 1919 Underground map was the first to include
the Johnston letters on a black bar across a red ring (top left); it
also appeared on a large station map poster (detail, top right). Two
trial designs from 1919 (second row), including one for rural General
services (not printed in colour before) were rejected. Johnston's
Proportions of Standard Bullseye Design (bottom) re-balanced the letters
and spaces and shape of the bar on the ring. This job was completed
in 1920 when the logo was registered with the numbers 659.834 and
.822 (still visible on some signs).

Contents

Foreword

Long before I even knew what typefaces were, they were influencing me. My first intimate relationship with type was seeing the text, usually accompanied by illustrations, in the books my parents read to me. I remember the friendly, comforting feeling of text that wasn't in capital letters and how, as I was being taught to read, it contrasted with the far sterner feeling of the capitals.

Although I remember being aware from an early age that type embodied feelings, I didn't yet connect feelings with the design of typefaces. But as I became a voracious reader, the distinct cover designs of yellow Rupert Bear books, red Just William books, *Swallows and Amazons* and *Biggles* soon became the graphic icons of my childhood. Then, as I entered my early teens and was abandoned, homesick, to the trains that took me to my remote school many miles north of Norwich, I remember the lettering used by the LNER railway brand and how good it looked to me on their wonderful steam engines and their glorious LNER posters. My interest in design, and in particular graphic design, was awakened.

I had no idea then that the LNER typeface had been designed by Eric Gill and that almost every word LNER needed to say was said in this one family of type. Nor did I know or care that among the typefaces I preferred then, and still do to almost any other typeface today, was the one that's still in use by Transport for London. With only minor cosmetic surgery, Edward Johnston's typeface is as clean looking now as it was when it was introduced in the late 1920s. Every time I see Edward Johnston's beautiful numbers on Thomas Heatherwick's

> # "The test of the goodness of a thing is its fitness for use"
>
> FRANK PICK,
> Design & Industry address,
> Edinburgh, 1917

brilliantly designed red double-decker buses I appreciate how modern, simple, clear and 'just right' they look today.

This illuminating and thorough book by Mark Ovenden will awaken all sorts of memories of urban life and literature in you. It will also open your eyes to the world around you. It is a wonderful account of the lives and work of two friends, two great type designers, and how powerfully their designs still influence the look of much graphic design in everyday life today.

Michael Wolff, September 2016

Michael Wolff, a founder of Wolff Olins, has spent more than 50 years helping organisations to affirm and express their identities. Working independently today, he's recognised as one among the world's most experienced and imaginative designers.

[1]

Frank Pick's most frequently cited quote is set in Johnston100 (see also pp 180–1 and headings throughout this book).

Gill Sans is: geometric

english

kinky

humanist

streamlined

overground

eternal

spiritual

artisan

modern

Introduction

A stroll along any British high street will reveal something rather curious about the lettering on view: almost all of it stems directly from, or shares some common ancestry with, the typefaces created by Edward Johnston (1872–1944) and Eric Gill (1882–1940). Indeed, their influence can be discerned throughout British life. Switch on the television or computer, open a newspaper, watch a film, read a map, fill in a form, go to a shop, take a train, drive along any road – almost everywhere you look, the lettering style they introduced will be there in front of you. And while this book focuses on Britain, their influence extends far beyond the UK – to Spain (Spanish government logos), Greece (signage at Athens airport), the former East Germany (road signs) and even the USA, for example, in the sets for the popular American series *House*.

Taking the reader on a chronological journey from the early 1800s to the present, *Johnston & Gill* first examines the style of lettering from which these two iconic typefaces emerged. With their clear and simple shape, sans serifs are deceptively modern-looking, though their roots stretch far back in history,

2
_____

Art director and graphic designer Peter Saville and typographer Paul Barnes of moderntypography.com made an exclusive piece of artwork for this book commemorating their thoughts of Gill Sans and the role the typeface has played in their work.

Johnston and Gill Sans feature on countless shopfronts along every British high street.

to the inscriptions of ancient Greece and Rome (p.43). From a faltering start at the dawn of the Industrial Revolution, to growing popularity in late Victorian Britain, sans serifs quickly gathered momentum, finding their crowning moment in the hands of two unlikely type creators: Johnston, a man of feather quills and Indian ink, and Gill, master of the stone chisel. Chapter 2 is devoted to their early lives, showing how, while neither was a typographer as such, both were consummate craftsmen, adamant believers in the appliance of hand skills over mechanisation, as well as friends and collaborators. Almost by chance – serendipity certainly played its part in the commissions they received, as subsequent chapters show – Johnston and Gill created a style of lettering that was to infuse the British psyche and which still endures today.

They did not produce their work in a vacuum, of course. In its overview of the history of sans serifs, Chapter 1 explains how the streets of the late 1800s and early 1900s were awash with posters and handbills (p.17), garish block letters vying for attention in an age before moving images and electronic advertising. Mass transportation, one of the fastest-expanding areas of the Industrial Revolution, threw up a million more signs and timetables, and the London streetscape in particular became such a jumble that the managers of the Underground were desperate to find a clearer, more authoritative style of lettering that would cut through the visual noise (p.24). It was against this backdrop that Johnston's calligraphy skills were called upon, and Chapter 3 tells the story of the build-up to the historic meeting between the visionary Frank Pick, of London Underground, and a reluctant Johnston. Ensuing chapters then show how, from tentative beginnings, a style of lettering emerged that would prove so effective and resilient that it grew not only to embody transport in the capital but became a sort of handwriting for London itself – one that celebrated its centenary in 2016/17.

When Gill was commissioned in the 1920s by the Monotype Corporation to design a sans serif for its state-of-the art typesetting machine (p.86), he could not fail to be influenced by Johnston's work. Gill had also studied lettering with Johnston and, with the zeal of a pupil determined to show his mettle, he strove to create a typeface that would improve upon that of his former teacher. Whether he achieved that is a matter of opinion, of course (p.105), but the typeface he produced was a runaway success almost from the word go.

Chapters 5 and 6 recount how Gill Sans was quickly adopted by the mainline railway operators (p.92) and distributed so widely to printing shops throughout the UK and Europe that by the end of the Second World War, and in the years of austerity that followed, it was arguably the most widely used family of letters seen in Britain. Chapter 7 traces the inexorable rise of Gill Sans, showing how its use by government agencies, nationalised industry and other institutions, from the Post Office to the BBC, led to its reputation as the (type)face of authority, conveying the very essence of Britishness. Neither typeface has rested on its laurels, however, and this book charts the meticulous revisions and adjustments that have been made to both Gill Sans and Johnston over the years to ensure that they remain up to date and fit for purpose, with Johnston100 and Gill Sans Nova making their entrance in the final chapter of the book.

Looking beyond its two protagonists, the book also introduces the new generations of type designers, both at home and abroad, who owe a direct debt to Johnston and Gill. From Margaret Calvert and Jock Kinneir – who themselves altered the very look of Britain's roads, railways, airports and hospitals (pp 150–1) – to the Swiss, French and German innovators of the 1950s onwards (p.147), every sans serif designer since Johnston and Gill has acknowledged their towering achievement. Stanley Morison (p.78) said in 1947, 'The Johnston Underground sans serif was the greatest single practical contribution that has been made to "good printing" in the last 30 years'.[1] And in 2015 Steve Heller of *Wired* magazine said, 'Gill's typefaces helped define England's commercial products and cultural landscapes'.[2] It is no exaggeration to say that, in the sphere of the written word, particularly in the presentation of advice and information, these two typefaces have performed the task for which they were created with unparalleled clarity, gravitas and style. Britons would be utterly – indeed, literally – lost without Johnston and Gill.

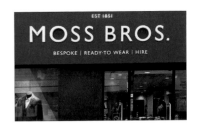

HOUSE *of* CASLON *&* J. M. Type Design

presents to you

THE FIRST EVER PRINTING SANS SERIF TYPEFACE

which was produced in about 1816 by

The Salisbury Square Typefoundry

which was owned by

WILLIAM CASLON JUNR

{THE GRANDSON OF THE FIRST WILLIAM CASLON}

This display sans serif went by the name

TWO LINES ENGLISH EGYPTIAN

this refers to the body size, equivalent to two lines 'English' type or about 28 points.

ABCDEFGHIJKLMNOPQRSTUVWXYZ

The revival was design and produced by

J. K. MARTIN LETTERFOUNDER

for

HOUSE *of* CASLON

1

A brief history of sans serifs

It's all about the pointy bits

What were the foundations from which Edward Johnston and Eric Gill developed a new visual style of letter? To understand this, it is helpful to take a look at the history of the sans serif. Derived from the French *sans* (without) and Dutch *schreef* (line), the term itself is descriptive, and it is not necessary to be a typography expert to spot the difference between a serif and a sans serif letter. The termination of any stroke (usually a straight line – for example, the left-hand side of a 'b' or the three straight legs of an 'm') provides the clue. If there is a small projecting line, or serif, at the end of the stroke, the letter belongs to a serif typeface; if it does not, then it is, by definition, 'sans' serif. In a serif typeface, serifs are used to finish off the endings of the strokes of a letter, it could be said, and the line forming the letter may vary greatly in thickness. It varies far less in a sans serif typeface, though even 'monoline' (that is, uniformly equal-looking) sans serifs are not precisely the same thickness throughout but are visually corrected so that they appear to be.

4 (opposite)

Jonathan Martin's 2013 revival of Caslon Sans in a poster for a university project illustrates the power and clarity of this first sans serif typeface, originally designed in 1816.

Type-specimen books were used to demonstrate wares: Figgins's from 1815 includes an Egyptian slab serif called 'Five Lines Pica Antique'.

FOUR LINES PICA IN SHADE.
FURNITURE,
FIVE LINES PICA ANTIQUE.
MANKIND
FOUR LINES PICA OPEN.
MAIDSTONE,
TWO LINES NONPAREIL ANTIQUE.
ABCDEFGHIJKLMNOPQRSTUVWXYZ,;:.-'
V. FIGGINS.

From ancient to modern

Sans serif lettering may have a clean and modern look, but its origins are in fact ancient, seen in carved inscriptions dating back to at least 500 BC. James Mosley, author of the definitive history of the sans serif, *The Nymph and the Grot* (1965), refers, for instance, to the 'monoline sans serif inscriptional letter of Republican Rome'.[1] There are also examples of early Greek lettering having been carved without serifs and, reaching back even further in time, what Mosley calls 'unstressed and unseriffed letters derived from Etruscan incised inscriptions'.[2] But this is not the place for a full history of hand lettering since antiquity up to the turn of the nineteenth century, nor an account of movable type since its invention in China around AD 1040. Neither can there be an in-depth examination of other influences that may have played a part, such as the raised lettering Valentin Haüy produced for the blind in 1786. The sans serifs that will be focused on here have their backdrop in the early 1800s.

Nothing was printed using a sans serif typeface before the 1830s, however, and after that for decades sans serifs were primarily employed only as display lettering, especially on posters, to make headlines stand out. They were rarely used for the body of the text because the relatively unvarying thickness of the line forming a letter gave a blacker effect on the paper, as if it had been set in bold. From the 1840s, however, there was what Michael Twyman, seasonal

CANON ITALIC OPEN.

CUMBERLAND.

CANON ORNAMENTED.

TYPOGRAPHY.

TWO LINES ENGLISH EGYPTIAN.

W CASLON JUNR LETTERFOUNDER

TWO LINES ENGLISH OPEN.

SALISBURY SQUARE.

6
———————

Somewhat confusingly, the first ever sans serif typeface was called 'Two Lines English Egyptian', the Caslon IV typeface from an 1819 Blake, Garnet & Co. type specimen.

lecturer and retired professor of typography at the University of Reading, has described as increasing 'use of different sizes and kinds of type to draw attention to specific elements within a text', including bold sans serifs.[3]

The term 'sans serif' itself seems to have been coined by type-foundry owner Vincent Figgins between 1828 and 1832, though it did not become common parlance among typographers until much later. In some early type specimens, it was spelled 'sans-surryph' (fig.10). Various collective terms have been used for sans serifs, depending on their characteristics (p.22): Egyptian, Ionic, Doric, Grotesque (the German term, often shortened to 'Grot'), Antique and Gothic, being the most common. Some of these can be seen in typeface names in use today, from Akzidenz-Grotesk (p.28) to Franklin Gothic (p.26), Grot No.9 to Antique Olive.

Print like an Egyptian

Its name reflecting the popularity at the time of ancient Egypt artefacts, Egyptian lettering in print can be traced back to at least the early 1800s, in the form of a joke book that seems to have been inspired by hand-painted lettering on London's streets. What is believed to be the earliest-surviving handbill printed in Egyptian lettering, and now in the British Library, dates from 1810.[4] Comprising blocky hand-painted serif letters that were completely squared off, Egyptian letters – sometimes nicknamed 'slab serifs' – must have appeared radical in a world dominated by serifs. But Egyptian slab serifs became increasingly commonplace in printing shops from this time, especially in the lucrative and competitive business of promoting lottery tickets, although some purists were allegedly outraged by the style of lettering.

Fuelled by the enthusiastic adoption of this distinctive form of lettering, foundries began to produce new type. Peckham-born Vincent Figgins (1766–1844), who started his career as a punch-cutter's apprentice in the 1780s, and his contemporaries the Caslons were key figures. William Caslon III (1754–1833), grandson of the celebrated typeface designer William Caslon, purchased the foundry set up by Joseph Jackson, a former apprentice of Caslon I, on his death in 1792. This was located in Salisbury Square, London. Helped by wealthy sponsors, Figgins started his own small foundry in Holborn during the same year. Achieving some acclaim for his work, he had produced a slab-serif typeface, complete with lower-case letters, by 1815 (fig.5).

The aesthetic appeal of Egyptian lettering lay in the fact that the words appeared much bolder (due to the more even stroke thickness). However, the slabby, chunky serifs were a bit of a distraction from the main architecture of a letter. An obvious move was to keep the uniform stroke width but shave off the serifs. This was first achieved – possibly as early as 1812 – by William Caslon IV (1780–1869), who designed 'Two Lines English Egyptian' (fig.6) at the Caslon Foundry in Salisbury Square, having taken over the business from his father in 1807.[5] Caslon's letters appeared, possibly for the first time, in a type-specimen catalogue from 1816, but the significance or usefulness of his radical new shapes was not immediately grasped – no examples of anything printed in this typeface during this period seem to have survived. As typographer Jeremy Tankard theorises: 'It failed possibly because it was too small, so it had no use for display – printers didn't know what to do with it.'[6]

Industrial Revolution drives the need for clarity

During the decade that followed Caslon's ignored sans serif, industrialisation was growing apace and new products began to be publicised in an early form of marketing. Advertisements started to appear on every available surface, from theatre playbills to shop windows, hoardings and railway wagons; they

sometimes covered the entire side of a building. Aside from being pushed into the hands of passers-by, leaflets were also pasted on to any and every available space. A few revealing images survive of just what a jumble some walls were, including Parry's *London Street Scene* (fig.7). Most signage was painted by hand, and almost always in capital letters, which to the modern eye might appear somewhat crude, even lurid, and definitely quite shouty. It was thrust into the faces of the new city dwellers of rapidly expanding industrial areas, from Glasgow, Liverpool and Manchester, in the UK, to Dortmund, Duisburg and Essen in Germany, and Baltimore, Philadelphia and New York in the US.

Nowhere was this more acute than in what was then the world's largest city: London. Already bursting at the seams in 1800 with almost a million inhabitants, and transformed by the arrival of the railways in the 1830s, the capital had doubled in size by 1840. Communicating with the new multitudes gave rise to a cacophony of written words all screeching for attention from the passing throng. What was needed was a neater, clearer, more authoritative shape of letter that could cut through the visual onslaught.

7
—————

A watercolour from 1835 by John Orlando Parry showing how playbills must have appeared in London's crowded streets. A popular singer and pianist, Parry may well have seen his own performances promoted in a sea of lettering similar to this.

Caslon

8

Caslon's sans serif from 1816 shown in the first modern printing from the matrices of the letters in Mortimer and Mosley's *Ornamented Types: Twenty-three Alphabets from the Foundry of Louis John Pouchée* (1993).

The significance of William Caslon IV's work in the history of sans serifs, and in the development of Johnston and Gill's own typefaces, cannot be overemphasized. The only letters printed from 1816 were the capitals produced in the type-specimen catalogue: 'W CASLON JUNR LETTERFOUNDER' (fig.6). Caslon's matrices, now stored in the Stephenson Blake files of the Type Archives at Stockwell, London, include some letters (such as 'G' and 'C') that were later re-cut. Figgins produced his sans serif in 1832 (fig.9), and given that it did catch on, and other foundries began making their own sans serifs, Caslon's 1816 lettering resurfaced.

The popularity of sans serifs — used in headlines and other display work — snowballed from the 1840s to a point where by the end of the nineteenth century they were almost ubiquitous. A key question for this book is to what extent Caslon's original 1816 designs influenced Johnston and Gill as they began to study lettering old and new. While there is no clear evidence that they would have seen the Caslon letters, according to Justin Howes: 'It is no coincidence that Johnston Sans bears a more than a passing resemblance to the very first sans serif type.'[7] Jeremy Tankard concurs that the Caslon Old Style 'underpins the geometry of the block sans'.[8]

The importance of Caslon's sans serif acquired new impetus in 1986. During their research for a book on the early, lost and forgotten ornamental typefaces from the Pouchée foundry, Ian Mortimer and James Mosley were alerted to a set of matrices of Caslon's Two Lines English Egyptian languishing in the drawers of the Stephenson Blake Foundry.[9] As it was facing imminent closure, they acquired them to make type from the moulds on an antique caster at Oxford University, using these to print the entire capital alphabet, along with several other sample texts in Latin (fig.8). Mortimer and Mosley presented the results in their book under the name 'Caslon's Egyptian'.

TO BE SOLD BY AUCTION, WITHOUT RESERVE; HOUSEHOLD FURNITURE, PLATE, GLASS, AND OTHER EFFECTS. VINCENT FIGGINS.

9

————————

Figgins's sans serif of 1832 in this 'Two Line Great Primer' size would equate to about 18pt in modern terminology, so was more practical for display purposes than the 1816 Caslon Sans, which was much smaller.

Mortimer was later commissioned to make new signage for the South London Picture Gallery in Dulwich. He and Howes copied the letters from the recast ones of 1986 and created a set of numerals and the resulting typeface was used for the wayfinding signage system at the re-opening of the gallery in 2000. A fitting tribute, as the original architect of the building was Sir John Soane (1753–1837), an earlier adopter of handwritten sans serif letter shapes for annotating his neo-classical drawings.

Other modern researchers have also commemorated Caslon's historic contribution. Take, for example, Jonathan Martin, who produced several variations of the entire alphabet for a university project. Shown in a documentary, *House of Caslon*, in 2013, it includes both an exact replica of how the fuzzy-inked edges of the letters may have looked (that is, the effect of ink squash and bleed as metal type impress on the paper) plus a cleaned-up version with highly defined edges (fig.4).

Although a direct link between Caslon and the work of Johnston and Gill cannot be established, the resemblance is striking. Indeed, it is worth flicking through these pages to compare all three alphabets. Although their work is considered Humanist (p.22) and these early faces were Grotesques – the letter 'C' being particularly characteristic – it still makes an interesting reflection. As Tankard says: 'I like to think of them as geometrics, different to the Continental idea, but still geometric: a softer, less rigid geometry – more "English".'[10] Given that Caslon's work was first published in 1816, and Edward Johnston's first alphabet for the Underground was commissioned by Frank Pick in 1916 (p.49), the year 2016 certainly had at least two significant sans serif centenaries to commemorate.

'Six, Five & Four Line Sans-Surryphs', from Thorowgood's 1832 specimen book.

Figgins had an idea to emulate the signwriters. Possibly inspired by Caslon's neglected type specimen of 1816, possibly just catching the zeitgeist, he built a heavier sans serif, which, with its thicker letterform, commanded more attention. First seen in 1832, the Two-line Great Primer Sans Serif was produced specifically for the purpose of printing powerful display letters (fig.9). Such is the fame of this typeface that it too has been digitally recreated by several current type designers, including Nick Shinn in 2008. His Figgins Sans also has lower-case letters.

From 'pica' to 'point'

In the digital age, when it is so simple to adjust something on screen, it is easy to forget that the moulds used to make these early typefaces had to be made from scratch for every letter, numeral and punctuation mark in each size of type needed. The modern measurement system based on point size was not yet in use in the early nineteenth century. British and American foundries in the 1800s referred to type size in terms of 'line' (two-line, seven-line) and pica (European foundries had different names for such classifications, like the French 'Didone', for example). There was no standardisation, so 20 pounds in weight of a particular typeface from one foundry would not necessarily match the exact size of the same weight of type from another. Without going into too much detail, a simpler way to understand what was meant by Caslon IV's Two Lines English Egyptian would be roughly equivalent to today's 14pt type size.

Among the various colourful names for measuring type, it was the pica that gained ascendency until the point size took over. The term 'pica', measuring one-sixth of an inch, was coined in the 1780s by the French printer François-Ambroise Didot; in France it was sometimes called a Cicero. It was represented by a capital 'P' with slash across it (₱). Point sizes did exist but varied from country to country and upon imperial or metric measures. It was not until the advent of electronic desktop publishing (DTP) in the 1980s that the DTP point was adopted globally. One point now is the equivalent of $\frac{1}{72}$ of an inch.

The sans serif sea

Caslon and Figgins were not the only type foundries around: Miller & Richard, based in Edinburgh, produced several Grotesques, while William Thorowgood,

11

The forward-thinking *Liverpool Mercury* changed its masthead in March 1834. As the typeface does not conform to any particular type specimen, it may have been produced especially for the paper, based on an existing face like Thorowgood's.

who had purchased the Fann Street Foundry from Robert Thorne in London, designed a full set of lower-case letters in 1834 for a sans serif that he called Grotesque (fig.12), arguably the first use of the term, in the UK at least. An early adopter, and one of the first journals to use a sans serif for their masthead, was the *Liverpool Mercury*. In its edition of Friday 7 March 1834, it switched from a more traditional hand-cut black-letter heading – based on Gothic script – to a modern-looking sans serif (fig.11). Though the typeface may not have come from Thorowgood's foundry (the exact provenance of the *Mercury*'s letters is unknown), the change would have appeared quite radical, marking the beginning of a transition to sans serif lettering for bold display words that would soon move into the ascendency.

Standing out from the crowd

A major application of sans serifs was for advertisements in journals, directories, newspapers and almanacs. Many examples from the 1830s onwards show how they were increasingly used for advertising, illustrating how they could stand out from serifs or slab serifs, especially where space was limited and the lettering was vying for attention with other text. In the writer John Lewis's collection of printed ephemera from the seventeenth century onwards,[11] some of the most intriguing examples of experimentation with sans serifs can be seen on throwaway items from the 1800s, ranging from invitation and trade cards, to exhibition notices and almanac covers. They would have been created using anything from wooden and metal type to wood blocks, hand engraving and hand-sketched letters.

Classifying sans serifs

Several attempts have been made to classify typefaces into groups, some with greater success than others, but it was the British Standard (2961) in 1967 that subdivided sans serifs into the four main groups: Grotesques, Neo-Grotesques, Geometrics and Humanists. These categories broadly comprise typefaces from a particular historical period, but recent typefaces can fit into any of the four categories.

The Grotesques

This group comprises sans serifs developed in the first half of the nineteenth century that were termed Egyptian, Antique or Grotesque (fig.12). Their main qualities are a vertical axis with stroke width that is almost uniform from end to end, though there can be mild variation. The ends (terminals) of curved sections are predominantly horizontal. In many, the 'G' has a spurred leg and the 'R' possesses a kind of curved leg. Almost all Grotesque capitals can be fitted into a square box (with some exceptions in very bold, thin or condensed variants). The height of the capitals and the ascenders of the lower-case letters usually match. Early sans serifs, especially the very first ones (serif lettering with the serifs shaved off), are also known as Realists. The Stephenson Blake Grot series, from the mid to late 1800s, is typically English. Later examples include Akzidenz-Grotesk (1896, p.28), Franklin Gothic (1902, p.26) and News Gothic (1908).

The Humanists

The defining characteristic of the Humanist typefaces, emerging from 1916 onwards, is that they deviate slightly from other sans serifs in having stroke widths that vary. They are said to be more calligraphic in style – less 'constructed', perhaps, possessing more flow, with a different rhythm in letter proportion and width, and a more 'classical' appearance. Looking virtually hand-drawn, the angle of the calligrapher's pen almost discernible, this is the family of typefaces to which both

Johnston Sans and Gill Sans belong. They were the first Humanists, effectively creating this category. Other Humanists include Granby (1930, p.106), Optima (1958), Transport (1963, p.151), Frutiger (1975, p.147), Bliss (1996) and Parisine (1998).

The Geometrics

Developed in the 1920s, and chiefly influenced by the German Bauhaus movement, these sans serifs are precisely geometric. Their most distinguishing feature is the visually perfect circle of the 'O'. The most well-known examples from this period are Erbar (1925, p.29), Futura (1927, p.122) and Kabel (also 1927). Avant Garde (1970s), Avenir (1988) and Century Gothic (1991) continued the tradition. They are the least employed sans serifs for body text, although typographical experts such as David Osbaldestein believe that Avenir works well for body text on screen.[12]

The Neo-Grotesques

Evolving in the 1950s from the Grotesques, and almost identical in stroke width to them, the main characteristic of these is the lack of embellishment in the terminals. A wide range of sizes and widths were developed to make them more adaptable for use in both headlines and body copy. Some critics argue that they have a somewhat plain appearance. Good examples of Neo-Grotesques are Univers (1954, p.147), Helvetica (1957, p.147), Rail Alphabet (1965, p.152) and Arial (1982, p.147).

Non-classifiable

Some sans serifs cannot be so neatly classified, however. URW Grotesk (1985), for example, exhibits both Geometric and Neo-Grotesque characteristics. There are others, with varied stroke widths, that can be mistaken for Humanists, but they may not always fit happily into that category for other reasons. Erik Spiekermann's FF Meta (1991), sometimes categorised as a 'Neo-Humanist Sans', has subtle stem and ascender curves and angled terminals. In recent years, a further subset, often termed Square, has emerged. This group – which includes Bank Gothic (1930), Eurostile (1962) and Neo Sans (2004) – can usually also be categorised as Grotesques or Neo-Grotesques, but they have a decidedly boxy appearance, especially in the lower case. In the view of experts such as Catherine Dixon, so much has happened since the digitisation of typefaces and the software to create them that 1960s classifications are in need of serious revision.[13]

12
_____

'Seven-Line Grotesque', one of Britain's first sans serifs, from Thorowgood's 1834 specimen book.

13 (top left)

The first sans serifs to appear in a railway timetable, issued by Bradshaw & Blacklock in 1839, marking the beginning of a trend.

14 (top right)

Sans serif signage on the architrave of London's Bayswater station on the eve of its opening in 1868.

15 (above)

The sans serif letters cut into the architrave on London's former General Lying-in Hospital have been dated to 1830, based on sketches from the time.

Signs for the times

The tumultuous explosion of railway construction in the UK during the 1800s led to the development and increased use of sans serifs, which began to be used in every aspect of the railway network, from station signage to timetables (fig.13). Since the 1820s the surveying and mapping of new lines, along with the designing and building of them, had been happening at breakneck speed, especially during the period of Railway Mania in the mid 1840s. It coincided with the emergence of many of the new sans serifs and proved a perfect pairing – a modern typeface for a brand new mode of transport.

The clearest photographs of sans serif signage on stations from this period come from a series dating from about 1868, on the extension of the world's first underground railway, the Metropolitan District, in London. Sans serifs were used from name signs on the platforms to condensed versions on architraves (fig.14) displaying the operating company moniker and letters pressed into concrete on the sides of bridges (fig.17).

This was not the first time that sans serif lettering had been cut into stone, of course, but it appeared to be part of a growing trend. Architect John Soane may not have followed his own lead by cutting into stone the sans seriffed lettering he used for annotation, but there are numerous other examples of inscriptions, especially on statues, where sans serifs were increasingly utilised from the late 1700s onwards. Mosley provides evidence of a handful of inscriptions in crude serif-free form that survive: one, for example, from 1793 in the Derbyshire church of St Oswald's in

An 1850 photo of a hand-painted *Standard Newspaper* advert in sans serif on the side of an early horse-drawn omnibus to Bank, London. Destinations were sometimes in sans serif lettering too.

Sans serif letters pressed into concrete formed this directional sign.

Ashbourne, and another by the sculptor and draughtsman John Flaxman (1755–1826) in Latin on a memorial of 1804. An early sans serif inscription that can still be seen is the architrave of the former maternity hospital on Westminster Bridge Road in Lambeth. The General Lying-in Hospital was re-sited to this location in 1828 and the name on the architrave was adopted by Royal Charter in 1830 when the sans serif lettering is thought to have been first applied (fig.15).

Signwriters and type founders

It would be a mistake to assume that this early chapter in the story of sans serifs is confined to printed ephemera and stone engravings: one of the key initiators of the style was undoubtedly the signwriter. It may even have been hand-painted signs that inspired the very first type without serifs. While shop, pub and hostelry signs were undoubtedly important sources of work, one of the earliest commissions for signwriters in the 1700s was painting lettering on canal boats. These mobile billboards were probably some of the most viewed, given how much of the country they traversed. Many of the first recorded examples resemble script, but with the serifs missed off, as has been surmised, for speed and ease of painting. A characteristic feature of early signwriting, one still seen on fairground rides, canal narrow boats and vintage shop fronts today, was a shadow added manually to sans serif lettering to give the illusion of a letter standing out – in 3D, as it were – something that would later be reproduced in type, such as the special face produced for the Festival of Britain (p.140).

18

Franklin Gothic, created for the American
Type Foundry in 1903, shown here in a
later type-specimen catalogue.

The term 'type founder' dates from the last few years of the 1700s, when the very first metal types were produced. Although foundries like Figgins, Dempster and Stephenson Blake exhibited examples of their letters in various catalogues, it is not thought that type-specimen books appeared until the 1810s. Even so, a study of these early catalogues illustrates how sans serifs were displayed to potential buyers (i.e. printing houses). Following a period of smaller foundries merging with larger ones, all the serif typefaces were shown together and all the sans serifs (usually forms of Grotesque at this period) were displayed next to each other – even if this did not show them to their best advantage.

Over in Germany, meanwhile, sans serifs were developing more quickly thanks to the many competing type foundries each making their own Grotesques, which led to more experimentation with weights and even lower-case letters – unseen in the UK at that time. Examples such as Breite Grotesk (p.28), Lilliput-Grotesk and Royal Grotesk were so versatile that they were not just used for display purposes. Their neat shape and smaller weights enabled them to be used for body text too.

Putting sans serifs on the map

It was from around the middle of the nineteenth century that sans serifs began to feature increasingly on maps. Established in 1791, the Ordnance Survey (OS) started producing the first printed maps of their trigonometric surveys in the early 1800s. Lettering denoting physical features and settlement names was drawn by hand in ornate seriffed lettering – with a handwritten or cursive appearance. Letters had to be written in reverse (apprentices learnt with the aid of mirrors) directly onto the copper engraving plates. Trying to simplify the process by using less fancy lettering led to some experimentation with sans serifs. James Mosley has unearthed cartographers' drawings dating from 1812 that label Roman settlements in a hand-drawn sans serif,[14] but it was not until 1833 onwards that maps in the OS First Series (established in 1805) began to include the lettering in print, with antiquities in particular captioned in a crude sans serif (fig.19). The practice was extended to the five-feet-to-the-mile (or 1:1056) series from around 1846. As sans serif lettering could theoretically be etched more quickly than cursive, the style was often also adopted for labelling the new railway lines that were proliferating across Britain, causing headaches for cartographers. In the fast-growing Midlands and northern cities, as well as in the London region, local boundaries were changing too, so it is no surprise that sans serifs were used both for labelling wards and large districts, with lettering that might spread across the entire map face. Used sporadically in cartography from the mid nineteenth century, notably on maps prepared for use on the Western Front during the First World War, sans serifs became far more prominent after the Second World War, with Gill Sans being introduced in 1953 (p.145), followed by Univers and Helvetica (p.147).

The twentieth century: a golden age of sans serifs

In a rapidly industrialising world, and with the expansion of advertising, by the 1890s virtually every printer worth their salt would have invested in sets of sans serif type. Among a variety of well-designed and popular sans serifs from this period several Grotesque typefaces emerged that may well have had an influence on the development of Johnston and Gill's work. The first of these, released in 1898 (itself honed by years of evolution – p.28), was Akzidenz-Grotesk. This was followed fairly rapidly by influential shapes of lettering from American Type Founders (ATF), whose head designer was Morris Fuller Benton. Probably inspired by some of the earliest sans serifs, Benton's Franklin Gothic of 1903 (fig.18), often compared with Akzidenz, also bears some similarities to Figgins's 1832 type (fig.8). It was popular with printers and by 1906 Benton had developed a condensed and extra condensed, with an italic in 1910. Further weights followed.

Other foundries made facsimiles of Franklin; these were produced both for traditional cold type and also for the hot-metal processes – for example, Barnhart's Gothic #1 and Linotype's Gothic #16 – and later there were many phototypeset and digital versions of Franklin and its variants. Benton also created a condensed sister face called Alternate Gothic in 1903, and a lighter, medium-weight version, News Gothic, in 1908. These were also emulated by other foundries, Linotype's Trade Gothic being one example.

The modern era

With the mechanisation of the printing process and the proliferation of sans serifs, it became increasingly important to be able to tell the printers what kind

19

The Roman road 'AKEMAN STREET', shown in a detail from an 1833 map of Oxfordshire, is one of the first printed examples of a sans serif on an Ordnance Survey map.

Akzidenz-Grotesk

Fette Accidenz-Grotesk

**Zum Goldenen Stern
EUGEN BINDER**

**Reklameschrift
BURGUND**

**Musik-Salon
EINBECK**

**Bundesrat
REIHER**

20

Type specimen of Akzidenz-Grotesk, designed in 1898, displayed in a type-specimen catalogue issued by Bauer.

German typefounder Ferdinand Theinhardt released a set of four sans serifs in 1880 destined for Berlin's Royal Prussian Academy of Sciences. Originally named Royal Grotesk Light, they were reissued later as Akzidenz-Grotesk Mager (light). (*Akzidenzschrift* is the German term for a display letter or a standard jobbing type.) Just a year later, another foundry, J. G. Schelter & Giesecke, produced an italic sans serif called Halbfette (medium) Kursiv Grotesk, and in 1882 the same company introduced a condensed version, Schlanke (condensed) Grotesk, but it was not until 1890 that Theinhardt designed the groundbreaking Breite (bold) Grotesk, sometimes referred to as the forefather of the modern Helvetica (p.147).

Another German company, Hermann Berthold of Berlin, was working with Bauer and Co. in Stuttgart and together they placed an advertisement in 1898 illustrating various sizes of a typeface they called Akzidenz-Grotesk (fig.20). There were ten fonts in the original release in light, regular, medium and bold (though no italics). Theinhardt's Berlin foundry was later acquired by Berthold in 1908, and the Swiss foundry Haas released their own sans serif, Haas-Grotesk, in 1912. Max Miedinger – the true father of Helvetica – is known to have regarded these early sans serifs as his inspiration.

Pioneering designers working within the De Stijl, Bauhaus and Dada collectives used Akzidenz, as did the 1950s Swiss and German designers (p.147), but one of the most striking ways in which the typeface has been used was in modernising the lettering on signage throughout the New York Subway in 1970. The project was undertaken by radical creative agency Unimark International, which included Italian designer Massimo Vignelli (1931–2014) and former Bauhaus artist Herbert Bayer (1900–1985) – both fans of minimalism. Recognising the need for a unifying look to rival the clarity of that achieved by the Johnston letters for the London Underground, they selected Akzidenz-Grotesk as the Subway typeface, which was not superseded until 1989 when it was replaced by Helvetica.

Erbar-Grotesk

20 P 1 - 12,10

Reichs-Handwerkertag in Frankfurt a. M. vom 6.-7. Juni 1939
Olympische Winterspiele 1940 in Garmisch-Partenkirchen

28 P 1 - 12,10

Deutsches Spring-Derby in München-Riem
Westfälische Drahtindustrie, Hamm i. Westf.

36 P 1 - 12,11

Die St.-Pauls-Kathedrale in London

a b c d e f g h ch i j k ck l m n o p q r s ſ t tj u v w x y z , . - ' : ; ! ? . ` * + ( ) „ " § à â á è ê é ì î í ù û ú
A B C D E F G H I J K L M N O P Q R S T U V W X Y Z Ä Ö Ü 1 2 3 4 5 6 7 8 9 0 È É É Æ Œ

21

The eponymous typeface designed by
Düsseldorf-born Jakob Erbar (1878–1935)
for the Ludgwig & Meyer foundry. The
first Geometric typeface, Erbar was based
entirely upon the circular 'O'.

of sans was needed. Typefaces needed to be classified (pp 22–3). Automated assembly of lettering can be dated to the late 1800s. The first machine employing cold-stamped type was the Philadelphia-based Lanston Monotype Caster, and by 1896 this evolved to a system that involved injecting hot metal into a mould. A competing US company, Mergenthaler Linotype, founded in 1886, developed its own system: the Linotype machine. Able to produce entire lines of pre-cast text from metal (slugs), it was initially dominant in the setting of newspapers. Monotype, which opened a UK branch in 1897, grew rapidly from simply supplying machines to commissioning typefaces for their own exclusive use. One of the major proponents of this, and an Arts and Crafts devotee, was its British typography consultant, Stanley Morison (1889–1967, p.78). Researching historic typefaces that could be adapted for modern use, he reissued Baskerville in 1923 as part of a successful revival programme. Morison was also aware of the rising popularity of sans serifs, particularly of German faces like Erbar (fig.21), and began looking for a British equivalent. It was his discovery of Eric Gill (p.86) that led to the birth of Gill Sans.

By the late 1960s/early 1970s, sans serifs dominated the graphic landscape. With the railways now arguably in their third age of sans serifs, the roads in their second – not to mention the health service, government and other bodies, which had all embraced the pared-back lettering style – it would have been impossible to move in any direction in the United Kingdom without being told how to get there, or what to do, by a sans serif typeface. This association in people's minds between sans serifs and official institutions has undoubtedly led to sans serifs being seen as representing the face of authority in Britain. Returning to the early 1900s, it was two typefaces in particular that were destined to make a major contribution to the universal adoption of sans serifs.

UNDERGROUND

BOOK TO · ·
PERIVALE · ·
SUDBURY OR
HARROW· · ·

FOR FIELD·PATH
RAMBLES IN·
OLD·FASHIONED
COUNTRY · · ·

CHEAP RETURN
FARES AND· ·
SPECIAL TRAIN
SERVICES ON·
SUNDAYS · · ·

St James'Park Station Offices. Dec. 1909.

2

An unlikely meeting of minds 1872–1914

Born in Uruguay in 1872 to a former army officer, Fowell Buxton Johnston, and his wife Alice, Edward Johnston spent his first three years abroad before the family returned to England. Back in the UK, and with his father looking for new employment, the young Edward was brought up in various rented rooms across the south of England, mostly in London. As cosseted children, kept away from schools for fear of infection, he and his three siblings were keen readers with a zest for learning, whatever the subject, from art and poetry to science. From a young age Edward attempted lettering text with a rudimentary quill, designing his own Christmas cards and producing copious sketches of cats. After receiving a book on the subject – thought by Priscilla Johnston, his biographer and youngest daughter (born in 1910), to be *Lessons in the Art of Illuminating* by Loftus[1] – 17-year-old Edward made an exceptionally fine piece of lettering on parchment for his aunt Maggie. It was shown to family and friends, and eventually to a local shopkeeper, Mr Whittingham, who believed it so precious as to be worth ten shillings. Whittingham also sold handmade Christmas cards by Johnston, the young man's first earnings from calligraphy.

22 (opposite)

Promoting the local countryside as a rural idyll, this 1909 poster for the London Underground by Charles Sharland encapsulates the Arts and Crafts style.

23

Cotton print (Compton) designed by William Morris from a 1934 Underground poster commemorating his centenary.

A year later, in 1890, the Johnstons moved to Plymouth, seeking healthier air for Edward's ailing mother, Alice. By early 1891 the family were back in London, settled in Hampstead, but Alice had passed away by the summer. This shock led Edward and his elder brother Miles (born in 1870) to consider a career. Miles went to study medicine in Edinburgh, while Edward gained a position as an office boy copying letters in an uncle's place of work at council offices in east London. At first he lodged in rooms at New Cross, later taking up residence at his uncle's home in Woodford. By 1895, Edward, his aunt Maggie, younger sister Olof (and the family cats) moved to Edinburgh, where they were joined by Miles. Here Edward prepared for university; he planned to study medicine too, although he did not much enjoy his year-long preliminary course.

The Arts and Crafts movement was in full swing at this period (pp 38–9), and it was in 1896, on a camping trip to the Lake District, that Edward read a journal article on illumination and became enthralled by what it had to say and by the work of Harry Cowlishaw (1869–1957) in particular. It was a pivotal moment, rekindling his interest in the art of lettering. His family had already noticed Johnston's lack of enthusiasm for medicine – especially dissection – not to mention his worsening health, blamed on the dank and draughty Scottish climate, and so it was decided he should quit the course and return to London. It was to mark a turning point in his life.

Towards the end of 1896, Johnston went to dine with family friends, the MacRaes, at Vernon Place, in Bloomsbury, London. There he met the MacRae daughters, Georgie and Mollie, whom Priscilla Johnston describes as unlike anyone her father had ever known.[2] Cosmopolitan and fun, they introduced Edward to the work of the Pre-Raphaelite painter Dante Gabriel Rossetti (1828–82) and to the textiles (fig.23) of William Morris (1834–96). With their artistic connections, they opened up a world of glamour and style that had hitherto passed him by. Edward wrote of the girls in his diaries: 'they are to my mind much more companionable than the very proper "ordinary persons"'.[3] It transpired that Cowlishaw was acquainted with the MacRaes, and Mollie showed him examples of Edward's work. In a letter to Edward, in which she described in great detail her meeting with Cowlishaw and his recognition of Edward's talent,[4] Mollie gave the young man all the encouragement he needed. It was this, combined with some cajoling from the only artist he had met in

Scotland – painter James Cadenhead (1858–1927) – that inspired him to return to the capital to embrace his artistic calling.

None of those close to him, and least of all Edward himself, had considered lettering as a career. At the turn of the century, calligraphy was effectively a dead art, with no one but Cowlishaw (himself a full-time architect), Morris, with an occasional foray into the subject, and a few enthusiastic amateurs, giving it the vaguest thought as a serious profession.

Reviving a lost art

Back in Edinburgh for a brief period, Johnston switched from medicine to an introductory course in drawing, which gave the 26-year-old his first qualification by March 1898. A few days later, in early April, he relocated back to London, with his family's blessing, to stay with the MacRaes in Bloomsbury. Within hours of his arrival, he was introduced to Cowlishaw and taken thence to Gray's Inn Square to meet the founder of the recently established Central School of Arts and Crafts, William Richard Lethaby (1857–1931). A friend of William Morris and sharing his rejection of the decorative art of the times, with its overly ornate and fussy style, Lethaby had been assisted in setting up the school for the London County Council (LCC) in 1896 by Morris.

Lethaby and Cowlishaw both advised Johnston to study early illuminated manuscripts at the British Museum. Cowlishaw also showed Johnston how to cut a goose quill correctly to create a broader nib. Johnston took to refining his skills with a newfound fervour. He had soon completed a manuscript of his own and took it to Lethaby, who offered to pay him 30 shillings for it. Before leaving, Lethaby informed Johnston that he intended to begin a new class on illuminating at the Central School. Johnston recalled that he was keen to be one of its first students, but Lethaby had another surprise for the young man: he wanted Johnston to lead it.

Protesting at first that he was unqualified to teach, but with the encouragement of Mollie and Cadenhead, Johnston consented. Before the new term started, he travelled to North America for a three-month trip with a friend, Neil McInnes, becoming fascinated by the modern urban electric transit systems (fig.24). Upon his return in September 1898, much boosted in self-confidence, he took a Bloomsbury bedsit, continued his studies at the British Museum and soon met

24

One of the North American cities that Johnston visited was Vancouver, where he was inspired by the city's electric street cars/trams.

God of Abraham · God
of Isaac, God of Jacob,
bless these thy servants, and
sow the seed of eternal life in
their hearts; that whatsoever
in thy holy Word they shall
profitably learn, they may in
deed fulfil the same LOOK,
O Lord, mercifully upon the
from heaven, and bless them.
And as thou didst send thy
blessing upon Abraham and
Sarah, to their great comfort,
so vouchsafe to send thy blessing upon these thy servants;
that they obeying thy will,
and always being in safety
under thy protection, may a-
bide in thy love unto their
lives' end; through Jesus
Christ our Lord. AMEN:

25

Johnston's 1899 Prayer of Blessing was
inked with a quill onto vellum.

again with Cowlishaw and Lethaby and their friends within the burgeoning Arts and Crafts network, becoming acquainted with the engraver Emery Walker and with Sydney Cockerell, a former secretary to William Morris and a leading authority on ancient manuscripts. Johnston later wrote in a letter to him:

> of three fixed *ideas* that had somehow become my own. These were (1) That there was something fascinating about lettering, (2) That letters were primarily intended to be read, and (3) that the forms of written letters would somehow properly depend upon the pen which wrote them . . . and so the idea came to make living letters with a formal pen.[5]

Johnston's own work progressed from what he described as his 'plain hand' to a more refined balance of letters and the spaces between them, and he produced many beautiful manuscripts, such as his 1899 *Prayer of Blessing* (fig.25).

Before Johnston delivered his first class, he worked even harder, earning some commissions for his lettering and displaying some of his work in public for the first time – at the Arts and Crafts Exhibition Society in the New Gallery, Regent Street. On 21 September 1899, he gave his opening lecture in writing and illumination – which he described as a 'practically lost art worth reviving'[6] – at Morley Hall on Upper Regent Street. As Johnston confessed to his first seven students, he was experimenting as much as they were. In its ramshackle building, the atmosphere of the new school was more that of a group of pioneers than any traditional teacher–pupil set-up. Attendees included Noel Rooke; Florence Kingsford – who later married Cockerell; Emery Walker's daughter, Dorothy; H. Lawrence Christie; T. J. Cobden-Sanderson (a friend of William Morris) and Walker's partner in the Doves Press, p.47); and Graily Hewitt. Soon after, the group was joined by a young heraldry student, Helena Hall. A former nursemaid to the Gill family, she would, two years later, encourage the young Eric to join her in the study of lettering, leading to the historic first meeting of Johnston and Gill.

Another class was soon started by Johnston in Camberwell and, in 1901, at the Royal College of Art in South Kensington. All his classes grew in popularity, his intense focus, painstakingly meticulous progress through each letter of the alphabet, with blackboards covered in chalked lettering, destined to become the stuff of legend (fig.26).

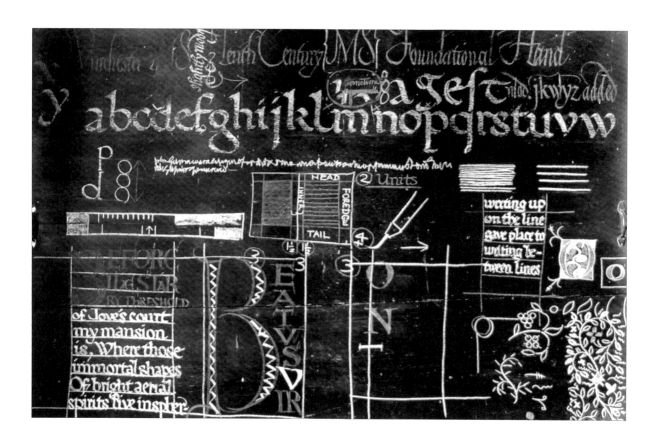

By the third term at the Central School, Johnston's class had progressed to the study of a famous monument from antiquity – Trajan's Column in Rome (p.43) – upon which had been incised, almost two thousand years earlier, letters in Roman square capitals (also known as majuscules), in a form of lettering visible on other ancient classical monuments, such as the Arch of Titus in Rome or the Parthenon in Athens. It was a style that would have great bearing on the way Johnston would later form his block letter.

Johnston attracts Gill

Johnston's generally tired demeanour, due to a sickly constitution, contrasted with his passion for lettering. This intensity appealed to the very soul of the 19-year-old Eric Gill. Born in Steyning, Sussex, in 1882, Arthur Eric Rowton Gill

26

One of Johnston's blackboards from his later classes, now in the collection of Central Saint Martins School of Art.

Johnston, aged 30, photographed with his
cat in 1902 at his Lincoln's Inn rooms.

was the son of a missionary clergyman, Arthur Tidman Gill and Cicely Rose
King. Gill spent his formative years in the Brighton suburb of Preston Park, in a
house that overlooked the railway, where he developed a fascination for trains
and locomotives. His brother Leslie MacDonald Gill, aka Max (pp 121–2) – one
of 12 siblings – arrived two years later. After a family move to Chichester in
1897, Eric attended the local Technical and Art School, moving alone to rooms
by St Saviour's Church in Clapham in April 1900 after being accepted as a
pupil in the practice of architect William Douglas Caröe in Whitehall Place.
Still a working practice today, W. D. Caröe specialised then, as now, in the
construction and renovation of ecclesiastical buildings. Gill commuted to work
via horse-drawn LCC tram or bus, wandering the streets of Westminster and
the abbey grounds at lunchtime.

Although Gill spent three years learning architectural drawing, his non-
conformist outlook was not best suited to the hierarchical structure of an office
and he felt constrained. Caröe wanted all his apprentices to enrol in additional
classes in architecture, but in true Gill style, and with the encouragement of
Helena Hall and fellow workers, he signed up for classes in stonemasonry, at
the Westminster Technical Institute (which became a school of art in 1904),
and also for Johnston's classes in lettering. The combination of what he learnt
in both was to send him in the direction of cutting letters into stone, for which
Gill would earn his first freelance income.

Early acquaintances of Gill's at this time included a fellow pupil of Caröe,
George Christopher Carter, with whom he became somewhat besotted ('his
mind was clear, his body beautiful'[7]). Gill saw him as a man of pure integrity,
and credits Carter with having introduced him to Edward Johnston. Carter died
young in 1907 and it was Gill who engraved his tombstone. The first of Johnston's
lettering classes that Gill attended, in 1901, marked the start of an extraordinary
personal and working relationship – some might call it a discipleship in its early
years. Gill became transfixed, recalling in his autobiography: 'I fell in love with
Edward Johnston and physically trembled at the thought of seeing him . . . as I
might, and indeed did [fall in love] with Socrates.'[8] The feeling must have been
mutual as Johnston and Gill developed a friendship that would last many years.
In February 1902, Gill went to have tea and a chat with Johnston in Lincoln's
Inn, where the latter was now living,[9] and Johnston, aware of Gill's misery at

the drabness of Clapham and the long commute, proposed sharing his rooms with the young architecture student (together with a stray black cat that had made the place its home). As Johnston wrote to his fiancée, Greta Greig, who was teaching in Wales at the time: 'I have been thinking about a plan to let a deserving architect have the other half of my bedroom . . . it will make a considerable change in my regime . . . I hope Mr. Gill will earn more money presently and that he will be able materially to reduce my rent.'[10]

By May, Gill had moved into Johnston's Lincoln's Inn lodgings. While it might have been an act of charity on Johnston's part initially – mixed with a little self-interest as an additional tenant would help pay the rent – to Gill the dramatic change in circumstances must have seemed altogether more momentous. Priscilla Johnston describes his dazzled ecstasy at the vaulted ceilings and historic character of his new surroundings.[11] Despite a number of heated debates, the pair were remarkably compatible. They entertained often – frequent visitors included Carter and two former students, calligrapher Graily Hewitt and Noel Rooke. Also often present was Ernest Treglown of the Birmingham Guild, who had been sent to London to learn lettering with Johnston – the two became great friends, Johnston refusing to take any fees for his tuition. Eventually Johnston was working closely with Hewitt (on lettering for an address for the coronation of King Edward VIII) and quite soon passing on commissions he did not have time for himself. Overall, however, this was a relatively carefree time for both Johnston and Gill, before work and married life took over.

Daily art and new horizons

Lethaby's Arts and Crafts-inspired outlook – that art is work, not meaningless beautification – was readily absorbed by Johnston and, by extension, Gill. Johnston boiled this down to the idea that the craftsman must be a workman, and Gill that the artist must lead an ordinary life rather than be cosseted like a hot-house plant. Despite, or maybe because of this, Johnston's progress on the book about lettering that he was supposed to deliver to publisher John Hogg by April 1903 was lagging seriously behind. It had been mooted back in 1902, but Johnston was so preoccupied with his classes and lettering commissions that he had to put off writing it. Another distraction was that he was engaged to be married later that year and he and Greta needed a home to live in.

28

Gill, aged 22, photographed in 1904.

William Morris and the Arts and Crafts Movement

Very little in life is free from the influence of what has preceded it. The formative years of Johnston – and equally those of Gill – were almost entirely dominated by a social and artistic group of radicals, coalesced around William Morris, and termed, in 1887 by T. J. Cobden-Sanderson, the Arts and Crafts movement.

In what was essentially a reaction to the decline in quality of the decorative arts and mechanised production methods during the late Victorian era, Morris, as a textile designer and leading proponent of the movement, believed that the artist should be a skilled craftsperson, designing and producing their works by hand. Continually referring back to the Middle Ages, and reacting strongly against the drudgery of factory work, he proclaimed that modern machines should be used only in the manufacture of artistic items when this might reduce the hours of manual labour needed and providing that there was no reduction in quality, which should always be of the highest standard.

His furniture and textiles celebrated the flora and fauna of the British countryside (fig.23) – some designs being left unfinished to enhance their rustic appearance. Morris insisted on mastering every aspect of the production process himself before opening the job to his staff. Paradoxically, his work became highly popular, giving rise to more mechanised production and spawning many imitators. Founded in 1875, the Liberty & Co. store was by the 1890s selling mostly Arts and Crafts goods. In 1891 Morris began the Kelmscott Press (fig.29) at his cottage in Hammersmith, publishing 66 volumes, mostly on vellum. The Arts and Crafts Exhibitions Society, formed in 1887, held five events up until Morris's death in 1896, attended by artists from across Europe, America

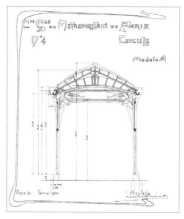

and the Far East. Meanwhile, France, Belgium and Germany were gestating a style of their own. Emerging from around the mid 1880s, with one foot in Arts and Crafts and the other in a fascination for Japanese art, by the time of the opening of the 1900 Exposition Universelle in Paris, the style had acquired a name of its own: Jugendstil, or art nouveau. By the turn of the new century in Britain, it was hard to find a corner of art, design, textiles, furniture, printing and architecture that was not at least touched by the Arts and Crafts, which – mainly thanks to Morris – had become strongly associated with the burgeoning socialist movement.

Arts and Crafts philosophy inspired architect Leslie William Green (p.50), and both Johnston and Gill. When it came to their block letters, they also owed a nod to the letterforms of art nouveau. Take, for example, the elegant 1903 lettering of Glasgow's Willow Tea Rooms, by Charles Rennie Mackintosh (1868–1928): clean and unadorned but with fanciful touches. It inspired Tony Forster to design the Willow typeface for Letraset/ITC in 1990 and for the same company to release ITC Rennie Mackintosh in Light and Bold in 2000. Art nouveau had also taken off far more in the form of the artistic travel poster (partly due to improvements in printing technology), the railways, and especially the London Underground, being among its greatest patrons.

So all-pervading were the Arts and Crafts and art nouveau styles at the turn of the century that neither Johnston nor Gill's lettering could have been immune from their influence. Indeed Gill's biographer, Fiona MacCarthy, goes further: suggesting that 'for Gill to see himself as the heir of William Morris would have been quite natural'.[12]

29 (above left)

The Kelmscott Press developed a distinctive imprint featuring calligraphic lettering designed by William Morris.

30 (above)

For the Paris Métro, art nouveau architect Hector Guimard (1867–1942) created the most exquisite structures – with his own flowing lettering.

Gill's clear, classically inspired serif alphabet
for W. H. Smith was much admired by
Frank Pick (p.55).

Johnston continued to put the book on hold and searched instead for new lodgings, which he found at Gray's Inn, leaving the Lincoln's Inn rooms to Gill, who brought in his brother Max as a co-tenant.

Gill's own interest in lettering was growing. Having cut almost a dozen inscriptions in stone by 1903, and created a Lombardic alphabet for use in Caröe's office, he gained a prestigious commission from architect Edward Prior to work on the pediment of the Cambridge Medical School building. This may have tipped the balance at work: he decided to quit architectural training and concentrate on monumental masonry, letter-cutting and calligraphy. One of his first commissions was for the Paris branch of British newsagent W. H. Smith & Son. Having painted the shop fascia on the rue de Rivoli at the end of 1903, he was commissioned by Charles St John Hornby, founding partner of W. H. Smith, to provide lettering for other stores around the UK. In 1907 he compiled his shopfront letters into a full alphabet for use in the production of in-store signage (fig.31). The alphabet for Smith's was not his first: in 1903 he was asked to design a title page for the Garden City Association publication as well as some lettering for advertisements by the Heal and Son department store in London's Tottenham Court Road.

Johnston's life was changing too. He married Greta, who had returned from teaching in Wales, on 20 August 1903, taking up residence in the Spartan new rooms at Gray's Inn, now full of Johnston's work paraphernalia and dominated by his big desk. Married life had put on hold the socialising of his bachelor days, but when Greta returned to her family home in Scotland to have her baby the following May, Gill, Hewitt and Rooke began dropping round again. Johnston and Gill took to walking up to Euston station to catch the late post (fig.32), their shared interest in trains reminding Gill of his enthusiasm for them as a young boy in Brighton. Johnston travelled up to Scotland for the birth of his daughter, Bridget, leaving Gill to deliver his classes for him in London, but soon returned, unaccompanied by wife and child, to continue work on the delayed book. It was something of a group project: Rooke would arrive to make sketches of Johnston's hands; Treglown was supposed to write an article on miniatures; Johnston had painstakingly cut out Trajan letters from photographs of the inscription to make up a complete alphabet; and Gill worked on an entire chapter. Yet by the start of the new term in September, the book was still not completed and Johnston had been separated from his wife and their newborn

32

Euston mainline station arch in 1896 (now demolished).

Pages from Johnston's book *Writing & Illuminating & Lettering* where he addresses the 'essential forms' of lettering, including the dangers of exaggerating the shape of the letter 'B'. Gill's 'A's, taken from his chapter in the book, are also shown. These shapes show evidence of the underlying structure of more elaborate calligraphy, but it is interesting to note their weight and balance when compared to Johnston's first drawings for Pick (p.60).

baby for the entire summer. It would not be ready until the summer of 1906, taking a total of almost four years from conception to completion.

Although not a fast seller, *Writing & Illuminating & Lettering* (fig.33) is widely acknowledged as a masterpiece – claimed by Sydney Cockerell, somewhat extravagantly, to be the best handbook ever written on any subject.[13] The effect it had upon Johnston was profound, a feeling of achievement that brought with it a sense of freedom. As Rooke observed, it had enabled him to improve his own calligraphy more in the six months following publication of the book than in the previous six years.[14]

Gill, at first somewhat downcast by Johnston's departure from their shared lodgings to get married, and the ensuing loss of their close male entourage, had discovered women for himself. He was married on 4 August 1904 to Ethel

Detail from the inscription at the base of Trajan's Column in Rome. From a photograph like this the letters were cut up and examples of each arranged in alphabetical order for a plate in *Writing & Illuminating & Lettering*.

Hester Moore (who took the name Mary upon their conversion to Catholicism in 1913). With a steady supply of stone-masonry commissions, plus the arrival of a daughter, Joan, in 1904, the Gills required more room. They moved first to a small flat in Battersea Bridge Buildings – leaving Max at Lincoln's Inn for a few more years. It was during this period that Gill met his first patron, Count Harry 'Graf' Kessler, who asked Gill to design the title pages of a luxury edition of Goethe. The Battersea flat was too small to hold a workshop for Gill and so he rented one, but the noise of his stone-cutting proved too much for fellow artisans in Upper Cheyne Walk, Chelsea. He began to search elsewhere, preferably for a place where he could work from home.

Reunited by communal living

The Johnston family, now back together again, were outgrowing the Gray's Inn rooms and looking for more spacious accommodation. The edge of Hammersmith, where it borders Chiswick by the river, had become the centre of a growing community of Arts and Crafts printers. Early in 1905, upon hearing that Emery Walker was about to vacate his home of 20 years, Johnston and his family took up residence at No.3, Hammersmith Terrace. Within a stone's throw of Walker, who had moved only a few doors up the road, and printer, writer and poet Hilary Pepler (1878–1951), along with the Kelmscott and Doves Presses, plus a river view and fresh air, this was an ideal location for the Johnstons – and for the Gills, who moved close by, to Black Lion Lane, later that year.

It was during 1904 that Johnston was introduced to Gill's patron, Kessler, for whom he was commissioned to design an inscription. Kessler encouraged Johnston to visit Düsseldorf to lecture the following year, but due to other commitments Johnston sent one of his best students, Anna Simons, who could speak German. She proved a fine ambassador, helping to inspire an interest in illumination, both through lecturing and through her translation of Johnston's book into German.

A page from Johnston's *Manuscript & Inscription Letters* showing one of the five plates by Gill that were included within the pack. The set was edited by Lethaby and produced in 1909.

Gill threw himself into the communal Hammersmith life and took his business to a new level. As well as employing a young lad to help move the heavy stones, he formed a partnership with another former Johnston student, H. Lawrence Christie. Johnston and Gill's closeness had been restored to almost Lincoln's Inn levels, though each now had his own family, and Pepler often joined them for trips to catch the midnight post or for deep intellectual discussion. Gill became quite the philosopher and a committed socialist, especially influenced by Pepler, with whom he started a working men's club in Hampshire Hog Lane. Johnston had also founded two groups: the Society of Calligraphers (known later as the Society of Scribes); and the Housemakers' Society, which sought to combat shoddy building practices. The latter was set up with Gill and its members included the writer H. G. Wells (1866–1946). By around 1906 Gill had developed into more of a teacher than a student, lecturing in lettering – often deputising for Johnston – and (thanks to a glowing reference from his former teacher) giving instruction in monumental masonry and lettering to stonemasons at the LCC's Paddington Institute, where he expanded on the sizable 'Inscriptions in Stone' chapter he had contributed to Johnston's book. Johnston, meanwhile, welcomed his second child, Barbara, during 1906, the same year that Gill's daughter Petra was born. Gill also joined the Fabian Society during that period, challenging their position on art, giving lectures and meeting such luminaries as the playwright George Bernard Shaw (1856–1950), becoming the society's typographical adviser for reprints of *Fabian Essays in Socialism* (first published in 1889) and producing stationery for the Fabian Arts Group. A ruckus during a 1907 demonstration put him off direct action politics, although he and Ethel attended a suffragette event in Hyde Park during 1908.

After the critical success of his book, Hogg commissioned Johnston to produce a portfolio of loose cards showing different alphabets based upon the lettering produced in his classes. Published in 1909 and aimed at helping to improve schoolchildren's handwriting, *Manuscript & Inscription Letters* (fig.35) anticipates the clarity of Johnston and Gill's block lettering to come.

Despite loving the proximity to his peers – including a brief affair and visit to Chartres Cathedral with Lillian Meacham, a fellow Fabian socialist – Gill was primarily a family man and felt London was not ideal for bringing up children. Park attendants would forbid the picking of flowers, for instance. He was also frustrated by the restricted living space at Black Lion Lane. So, in the summer of 1907, the family moved to the rural village of Ditchling, near Lewes, in Sussex, a location that was to prove central to both him and Johnston. The modest old house called Sopers on the High Street 'had an entrance hall that wasn't a mere passage . . . and a great big kitchen big enough to have family meals in'.[15] Johnston and Gill had both discussed moving out of London – Chichester was mentioned – and several of their artistic friends had left the capital too, but the South Downs, including Ditchling, were also in Gill's blood from infancy. Johnston was simultaneously spreading his wings: based on the popularity of his book, he was beginning a series of lectures in Manchester, as well as working long hours each day on Robert Browning's *Men and Women* for the Doves Press.

Gill continued to commute regularly from Ditchling to London for inscription jobs or woodcut lettering commissions, spending much time with Alfred Richard Orage, co-founder of the Leeds Art Club, a centre of modernist culture, and publisher of the *New Age*, for which Gill did the masthead in 1907 and to which he also contributed articles. Gill was moving in different circles now, becoming fixated with the concept of good construction over all else: sculptor Jacob Epstein (1880–1959) and painters Roger Fry (1866–1934), Augustus John (1878–1961) and William Rothenstein (1872–1945) became his new acolytes, and his adherence to the Arts and Crafts movement was diminishing – he was even lecturing on what he perceived as its theoretical faults. Although almost all of his work concerned lettering in its many forms, and he still required apprentices and assistants to help him complete all the jobs – one of whom was the sculptor Joseph Cribb (1892–1967) – by late 1909 Gill had completely embraced sculpture. He was also influenced by the philosopher and historian Ananda Coomaraswamy (1877–1947), who helped found the Indian Society. A collector of exotic and erotic works from the Indian subcontinent, he was responsible for introducing them to the West. It was Indian temple sculpture in particular, and the overt sensuality of the entwined figures, that fascinated both Gill and Epstein and shaped their work. Gill's third daughter, Joanna, was born in 1910 when Epstein came to work at Ditchling on the tomb for Oscar Wilde (now rehabilitated in the eyes of the public after his death in 1900), with an inscription designed by Gill. It was the following year, January 1911, that Gill held his very first sculpture exhibition, at a gallery in Chelsea.

Johnston was also expanding in other directions: the 1910 Arts and Crafts Exhibition included a book of wild flowers illustrated by Olof, for instance. He was making more trips out of London, too. During 1911–12, he stayed at the Peplers' Dorset cottage and frequently visited Gill at Ditchling, where, on one visit, they conceived the idea of an artists' community, with living accommodation and workshops arranged around a central quadrangle. The Johnstons finally moved to Ditchling in October 1912 – not to a communal house, but to a redbrick villa at the village edge, with a view of the Downs. Since it was a mile and half's walk from the station, Johnston had to give up all his classes in London, with the exception of the original one by then transferred to Royal College.

In the summer of 1912, despite Gill's antipathy to mechanisation, he developed an unlikely affection for an impetuous and dynamic printer called Gerard Meynell (1878–1960), who later went on to found the prestigious Westminster Press. In January 1913, along with typography expert John Henry Mason of the Doves Press and lithography specialist Francis Ernest Jackson, Meynell and Johnston started a journal of printing and book production (fig.36), to be known as *The Imprint*. Covering subjects from lithography to typography, and with a serif typeface designed by Lanston Monotype for the journal (Series 101, 1912) so that it could be set on the company's new caster (p.86), it lasted for only nine issues due to differences between the four co-editors. Meynell none the less visited Ditchling often and eventually brought his family to the village too.

Between 1912 and 1913, Kessler commissioned Johnston to design type for the Cranach Press, though he had to pass the work on to Gill to complete. Johnston believed the proper person to design type was the punch-cutter but came to terms with the idea by seeing it as a collaboration between the masters of that profession and himself as a calligrapher, skilled in designing the actual look of the letters. Kessler then commissioned Johnston to work on a black letter for a version of *Hamlet*.

The years 1913–14 turned out to be a pivotal period for both Johnston and Gill: Gill began work on 14 panels for his *Stations of the Cross* at Westminster Cathedral. Johnston, having finally moved to Ditchling, and the Gills having also relocated out of the village to Hopkins Crank, a plain but sturdy house on the edge of Ditchling Common, took a step towards realising their proposal for more communal living when Gill built himself a workshop alongside the house. It was during 1913 that Gill first came across Stanley Morison, with whom he was to work closely in later years (p.78). Gill also produced an alphabet for a book called *The Ship Painter's Handbook*, published in 1915 (p.59). The Gills, and possibly by association the Johnstons, also became friends with yet more of Britain's literati – Leonard and Virginia Woolf. But more important than any of these notable achievements, as will be seen in the next chapter, was the fact that Meynell took Johnston to a meeting at the headquarters of the Underground on 16 June 1913 that would transform the lives of both himself and Gill, not to mention the whole history of typography.

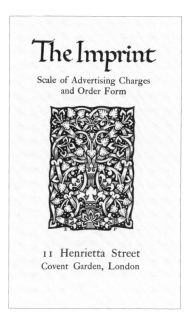

36

Johnston's hand-drawn masthead for *The Imprint* from 1912–13, reproduced on a rate card for advertisements.

TOO MUCH OF A GOOD THING

EVERY VARIETY OF
PLEASURE RESORT.

PARKS & PLAYGROUNDS
RIVER-SIDE
COUNTRY-SIDE
SEASIDE
PALACES & GARDENS.

ELECTRIC RAILWAY HOUSE, BROADWAY, WESTMINSTER.

JOHNSON, RIDDLE & Cᵒ LTD. LONDON. S.E.

3

Pick's new face for London 1915–16

In the first years of the twentieth century, what was to become known as the London Underground expanded substantially, with four new lines burrowing beneath the West End and the City. Great strides were made in publicising and branding the system, but it all lacked the unified feel that was sought. In an effort to redress this, a commission was about to be made by the Underground owners that would prove fundamental to both Johnston and Gill.

The first of the new services to open began running in 1900. The Central London Railway (CLR) was operated independently. Inspired by the successful design of the first electric line (the City & South London, CSLR, opened in 1890), it utilised similar white tiles for its station platforms and passageways and borrowed from the Metropolitan and District lines (and the main lines) for station-name signage, using bold sans seriffed capitals on long wooden boards with a black background. Enamelled signage for 'WAY OUT' signs also employed a crude sans serif. Advertisements and ephemera utilised yet more sans serif typefaces and lettering styles (fig.37).

37 (opposite)

A 1909 Underground Electric Railways of London (UERL) poster extoling the virtues of its own advertising, all redolent of Arts and Crafts design influences and lettering.

38 (above left)

At London's new stations, where there was no space for a building, entrances were little more than a hole in the ground with some railings around the stairs (as here at Oxford Street, now Tottenham Court Road). Lettering in bland sans serifs did not even hint at Leslie Green's decorative work below ground.

39 (above right)

South Kensington station, photographed in 1907, showing a mixture of different lettering. Leslie Green's seriffed sign for the station appears on the central architrave, the line name shown in a different seriffed face on the sign above and an enamel panel, 'FAST ELECTRIC TRAINS', in a generic sans serif. This mishmash of different styles was becoming an issue for Frank Pick.

Green introduces a more unified style

Between 1906 and 1907, three more lines were opened that would later become the Bakerloo, Piccadilly and Northern. These fell under the control of the bigger conglomerate known at this stage as the Underground Electric Railways of London (UERL, also called 'the Combine'), which was funded by American Charles Tyson Yerkes. The company architect Leslie Green (1875–1908) was charged in 1903 with designing over 50 station sites from street level to platform. An Arts and Crafts devotee, Green liberally employed the style across every aspect of his work for the Underground, from ticket halls to station name signs (fig.40). It is even possible that, had Green not died prematurely – possibly due in part to the stress of having to build so many stations in such a short space of time – he might have been asked to develop his style into an alphabet to be adopted by the entire network, though design historian David Lawrence thinks this is unlikely.[1] Seriffed lettering in Green's stations would be superseded by Johnston's work, but thanks to staunch efforts by conservationists, some of Green's original designs are still visible today. According to Doug Rose, who has made a study of the coloured tile patterns,[2] there was a conscious effort to give each of the sites a cohesive look. Rose believes that the only mild variation between the exact shape of the letters was down to the four different ceramic companies involved in their production.[3]

Gibb brings Pick on board

After Yerkes's death in 1905, the UERL was chaired by the philanthropist Sir Edgar Speyer, another Arts and Crafts aficionado. In 1906 Speyer appointed Sir George

40

Signage from street level to subterranean platform at one of Green's Arts and Crafts-inspired stations. From top to bottom: gold-relief capitals on the architrave of Holloway Road's classic 'ox-blood'-coloured tile exterior; the ticket hall with its raised lettering on a booking-office window; a cartouche frieze; a passageway sign with flared directional arrows; the station name emblazoned in foot-high letters on the tunnel wall.

A portrait by Patrick Larking (1907–81) of Frank Pick in his later years, during his tenure as London Transport Chairman.

Gibb, previously general manager of the respected North Eastern Railway (NER), as UERL general manager and deputy chairman. Gibb brought his young assistant from the NER, Frank Pick (1878–1941). Although he trained to be a lawyer, Pick was showing a flair for traffic management and by 1908 he had been promoted to the role of publicity officer. Working alongside Albert Stanley, managing director from 1910 and company chairman by 1919, he began to develop a unifying visual style for the London Underground that would include the iconic bull's-eye (which would nowadays be called a logo) and the look of the stations themselves.[4] Indeed, it was Pick's keen eye for design, his insistence on a consistent style, and his commissioning of new artists that later led him to becoming one of the founder members of the Design and Industries Association (DIA) in 1915. Paying close attention to lettering from the outset, Pick first of all strove to push up passenger numbers by focusing on printed ephemera.

Pick's publicity drive

Although the Metropolitan, CLR and several smaller lines were not at that stage part of the Combine, in 1907 the overarching word 'UNDERGROUND' had been chosen as a corporate name for the UERL lines. A logotype had been adopted – an enlarged initial 'U' and final 'D' – with the smaller middle section, 'NDERGROUN', often displayed with dashes above and below each letter. There were also slogans: 'UNDERGROUND TO ANYWHERE', 'QUICKEST WAY', 'CHEAPEST FARE'. Pick, who was put in charge of UERL publicity in 1910, began to commission commercial artists to produce bright and colourful posters, incorporating these slogans, to encourage passengers to use the system outside the rush hour to visit countryside attractions. Most of the early poster designers were sympathetic to the Arts and Crafts movement, including artists such as Walter E. Spradbery (pp 57–9), Charles Sharland (p.65), Alfred France and John Henry Lloyd. Later commissions drew in more avant-garde designs, including American Edward McKnight Kauffer (1890–1954), one of the most influential graphic designers of his time.[5] Artists were either given direction by Pick to produce freestyle lettering on the posters, or it was added by the printing house – resulting in vivacious variations in style.

The posters certainly had the desired effect of brightening up the platforms and increasing passenger numbers, but UERL's stations themselves now ranged from some of the most modern designs to a ragtag collection of often quite

42

In this poster from 1908, John Hassall was commissioned to produce just the artwork, including the 'P'liceman' and Leslie Green's characteristic ticket hall décor. The large 'U and D' logo, silhouette skyline and slogans on either side were added by Pick's publicity office in one of the first attempts at conveying a corporate identity for the Underground group.

43 (left)

Of Pick's early bar and circle devices for station name signs a handful still survive, like this one at Ealing Broadway. The lettering was usually a squeezed sans serif, here bearing some similarity to Franklin Gothic Condensed (p.26).

44 (right)

One of the photographs from Pick's 1907 station survey with a new large 'U and D' logo inked onto the image – along with a series of poster frames and map-holders.

shabby buildings dating back to the 1860s. What was now desperately needed was something to pull all the improvements together. Pick asked commercial artist John Hassall to come up with a design for a poster that would enable him and his team to bring together some of the disjointed elements – from the station architecture to the Underground's trademark 'U and D' logo (fig.42).

As part of the drive, Pick commissioned a photo survey of every station exterior. His engineers then superimposed in ink on each photograph examples of how the new logo – with the letters presented vertically in a sort of totem pole – might look alongside specially cleared spaces for poster frames and maps of the system (fig.44). These totems, signs and frames were made up by signwriters, across Britain, all by hand, using fairly basic, non-specific sans serif lettering – although there was some guidance from the drawings. They were erected around London on each of the UERL's sites. Pick also focused on the station signage, introducing a bar and circle device for station name signs, with 500 being installed on platforms throughout the Underground system (fig.43). But he must have been frustrated that, despite the improvement in visibility in the streetscape, there was still a distinctly uneven, and in some cases positively chaotic, appearance to many of the stations with such a mixture of signs and letters.

The need for a new alphabet

A similar process was happening with Pick's inspiring array of posters. While they were mostly strikingly colourful and inventive, they too lacked consistency, mainly due to the lettering. Pick started discussing the issue and would have been aware of the growing influence of Johnston's calligraphy classes. Having seen and admired Gill's Trajan-based seriffed lettering for W. H. Smith (p.40), he wanted something with this level of gravitas for the Underground but not too alike, to avoid a potential clash given Smith's kiosk presence at stations. So he had in mind a block or monoline letter, feeling that it would look better on flat surfaces than a seriffed one and preferring the simplicity and clarity it offered in a visually 'busy' environment.

In effect, Pick had been contemplating the need for a new alphabet to be used on all the printed material – especially the posters. He was looking for a style in which each letter in the alphabet must be a strong and unmistakable symbol with a high degree of individuality.[6] He also stipulated that each letter must be clear and open. Since the lighting on the station platform was likely to be less bright than the lighting in the train, it must have the greatest possible carrying power. It must be straightforward and 'manly' with the character of an official railway sign that was not to be mistaken by people in a hurry for the trade advertisements.[7] A myriad lettering styles jostled for attention on timetables, notices and posters, so Pick needed to find the elusive letter shape that would sum up the modernity and authority required for a mass-transit network in what was then the world's biggest city. As his biographer Christian Barman comments, Pick 'was looking for a typeface that would belong unmistakably to the times in which we lived'.[8] Priscilla Johnston, meanwhile, observes how he 'experimented with compasses and the set square, aiming at an alphabet based on squares and circles. He was looking for someone to embody what he had in mind.'[9]

Pick's drive for modernisation found resonance in company architect Harry Wharton Ford, who was responsible for the District Railway and had played a significant part in the development of the bull's-eye station name signs (fig.43). According to David Lawrence, Ford's role has been underemphasised and that it was he who drafted 'a seriffed font for station exteriors, and a block letter for station signs'. Indeed, it was Ford's block letter (fig.45), in his view, that 'added impetus to the search for a universal Underground lettering system'.[10]

The block letter is discussed

Pick's designers and printers were coming up with their own lettering styles, all of which he would have overseen to some extent. He had also commissioned

45

Wharton Ford's block lettering on a station name board at South Kensington. In 1908–10 Ford employed two types of sans serif at District line stations: a condensed blocky serif for platform signage and a less condensed version for the exterior, such as on canopies. Made by different manufacturers, they would not have been identical and sometimes the condensed versions were even used interchangeably.

a colleague of Johnston, *Imprint* co-editor Francis Ernest Jackson, to make a poster (of Chiswick Mall) in 1913. Of particular interest to this story are a set of Tramway posters by Walter E. Spradbery that appeared in 1913 and which may well have played a role in Pick's thinking (figs 47 and 48).

One of Pick's favoured printers was the Westminster Press and over the years he had developed a relationship with its founder, Gerard Meynell. In June 1913, with the encouragement of Meynell, with whom he discussed his lettering issues, Pick managed to get the reluctant Johnston to meet him for the first time. (Gill had just started working on his biggest commission to date, *Stations of the Cross*, so would not have been available.) Any details of their discussion no longer remain on record, but since it is known that Johnston did not start work for Pick at this stage, it must be assumed he was not inclined or able to take on the commission then. Pick, however, must have been urging his poster designers to improve the lettering. A number of examples of a clear block letter dating from between 1913 and 1915 suggest that, even without anyone to design a new alphabet, he was striving for something authoritative (fig.46). Pick met again with Johnston on 29 October 1915. This time Gill was also present and, as Johnston noted in his diary, they discussed block letters for the first time.[11] Recalling the meeting at a later date, Johnston remembered Pick making reference to the exhaustive research he had conducted to arrive at the ideal block letter. In the biography of her father, Priscilla Johnston records in some detail Johnston's calculations based on Pick's requirements:

> the basic idea of this Underground alphabet (block letter mono-stroke being the only prescribed condition) was to combine the greatest weight for mass with the greatest clearance of letter shape. The lower-case 'o' is the key letter: it is circular and has a counter equal to twice its stem-width (giving approximately ideal mass and clearance): its height is four stem-widths and the shortest (or approximately ideal) ascender or descender projection equals three stem-widths, giving seven stem-widths for the 'b', 'd', etc. and hence for [the] capital A, B, C height.[12]

Johnston refined these calculations later, in 1934, when he realised that he had made some errors in his original estimates.

46 (left and below)

Sans serif lettering on three different posters by P. Cottingham, 1915–16. They were printed by Johnson, Riddle & Co. Ltd, and must have been seen by Johnston and Gill when discussing block letters that year. The similarity of all this lettering to the work being undertaken by Johnston at precisely this time cannot be overlooked.

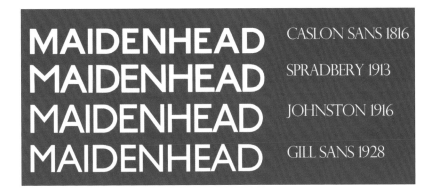

47 (left)

Comparison of the 'MAIDENHEAD' lettering from Spradbery's poster (fig.48) reveals much in common between it and Caslon's 1816 alphabet (p.18), Johnston's first alphabet for UERL (p.60) and Gill Sans Titling (pp 91, 95 and 104).

ABCDEFGHI
JKLMNOPQ
RSTUVW&
XYZ

Johnston and Meynell attended a further meeting with Pick, on 8 November 1915, and although Gill was absent, he noted in his diary that 'Johnston came to tea on his return to Ditchling to discuss the lettering and the fee of 50 guineas which Pick had offered for the job'.[13] The two were often in and out of each other's homes — as was Hilary Pepler, who had moved to the village in 1915 — and would also have been involved in discussions given his print background. The Underground project had also come at the same time that Johnston was assisting Pepler with the printing of one of the Gospels in Caslon Old Face. Even if Johnston had not come across Caslon IV's 1816 sans serif before then, it is possible that he would have done so during this project with Pepler. Either way, typefaces and discussion of them were in the Ditchling air.

Despite Johnston's commission from Pick, (Gill was totally absorbed in his sculpting, especially the work for Westminster Cathedral, and so was unable to give the Underground alphabet his full attention), Johnston still gave Gill 10 per cent of the 50 guinea fee for his contribution. However, although Gill left the job to Johnston — partly due to his own projects but also, as Priscilla Johnston implies, partly because Johnston was not easy to collaborate with — it is known that the pair discussed progress over communal meals at Ditchling. In his work on the *Ship Painter's Handbook* (fig.49), and as a reaction to being told that 'there are no good types of block letter in use by printers',[14] Gill had made some sketches of his own for a monoline or block letter and these undoubtedly had an influence on Johnston's initial designs.

Following the outbreak of the First World War, 1915 was a year characterised by human tragedy and it weighed heavily upon every aspect of life. Despite being given only until the end of the year to finish the project, Johnston did not

OUR TRAINS ARE RUN BY
LIGHTNING
OUR TUBES LIKE THUNDER
SOUND
BUT YOU CAN DODGE THE
THUNDERBOLT
BY GOING UNDERGROUND

51 (left)

In February 1916, Johnston submitted this draft for a trial poster. Though it appears a little untidy – it was after all just a test – it impressed Pick sufficiently to press Johnston for revisions.

52 (below)

Johnston's fascinating 'first drawing' with five 'W's (the first, on the second line, was used until the late 1930s). The first three letters on the third row are also striking: the 'S' disappeared after this draft, but Gill liked it and his own 'S' (p.83) is similar. The 'J' has a boot that is so highly calligraphic that it borders on a serif and was modified by Johnston (fig.53), as was the idiosyncratic 'G', which stayed on the second draft though a terminal pointing inwards was added later (fig.54). All Johnston's and (subsequently Gill's) capital 'G's were 'beardless' – i.e. without the supporting leg that the Neo-grotesques mostly all have (as in the Helvetica 'G'). Both Johnston and Gill preferred the middle apex of the 'M' be at the centre of the letter as opposed to hitting the baseline.

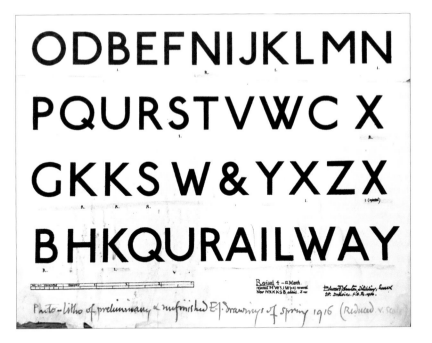

53

The second draft (March 1916) included changes to or replacements of 12 letters (and notes added in pen by Johnston). Gone are two of the five 'W's – although one was later brought back and became the final version. Alternative versions of both the 'K' and 'X' went up from two in the first draft to three here. The 'S' from the first attempt is replaced with another trial version (on the third row), which never went any further. Also missing were Johnston's quaint but untidy attempts at punctuation, which on the first draft were clearly based on pen strokes rather than type design. Johnston also submitted his first lower-case letters, which included a rather peculiar 'g' and second 'q', no 'f' or 't' and no tittle for the 'i' or 'j'.

ODBEFHIJKLMN
PQURSTVWCG
QU WA &YXZJ

Notes of details (in case of
Some being overlooked or
in case of slight inaccuracies)
Note : the 2nd QU to be cut together on one body

height of letters = 1
width of stem = ⅟₇ th.
(the curves of (B) are
slightly less than ⅟₇ th.)

OQCGS& are a little taller than 1 and project
slightly above & below top & foot lines.
J projects slightly below foot line
K top arm K'e W center W fall slightly below top line

WITH CARE, INK NOT waterproof.

Revised 4 –12 March.
rejected H W S J W (EA) removed
New N X K K S B added. Z cut

Edward Johnston Ditchling, Sussex
1st. Drawing. F.o. Fe. 1916

Johnston's drawing of June 1916 for the finished upper case is a thing of beauty in itself. Not simply because it was the model from which the Underground alphabet was mechanically reproduced, but also because Johnston painstakingly cut out and pasted on revisions and left evidence of the evolution of his work – for example, the pencil marks on the letter 'G' (now resplendent with a new inwardly pointing terminal) and the compass marks in the middle of the 'O', 'Q', 'C' and 'G'.

feel able to tackle the alphabet for Pick seriously until some time after their 8 November meeting. It was not until mid December that he produced his first six capital letters, 'B', 'D', 'E', 'N', 'O' and 'U', at two inches in height. Although only one of these letters has survived (fig.50), its similarity to Gill's *Ship Painter's* block letter, and the lettering Pick was demanding for certain posters, is quite striking.

Pick was not keen on the petits-serifs, however, so Johnston recommenced work early in 1916, removing the serifs entirely and redesigning the 'B', 'D', 'E' and 'O' at the one-inch height in which the letters would be required for the final submission. The entire alphabet was ready by 6 February 1916 (fig.52) and submitted first to Meynell, then to Pick. It was lithographed and discussed by Pick and the publicity office and a trial poster was assembled (fig.51). Although, as Howes suggests, Johnston's first draft shows 'little evidence of hesitation'[15] and has an undoubted confidence about it, Pick none the less insisted on several alterations (for example, the 'H' in the first line, which was deemed too wide by

Pick, like those on Spradbery's posters, p.58), and a second draft was prepared by March 1916 (fig.53).

Johnston's drawings for the second submission were also lithographed and discussed at length by Pick and colleagues (and possibly tested on trial posters too). Meanwhile, Johnston was hard at work on the lower-case letters, the numerals and the punctuation. The survival at the St Bride Library of a second, unfinished, drawing for the lower-case letters – dated 13 March, just one day after his work on the capitals – suggests that he must have been working simultaneously on both. After incorporating comments from Pick, Johnston submitted his finished design for the upper-case letters on June 1916 (fig.54) and the final design for the lower case a month later (fig.55). As Howes points out, the next part of the process would have been somewhat alien to the calligrapher Johnston.[16] Indeed, had it not been for a missing letter and some of Pick's other pressing needs, the year 1916, as will be seen in the next chapter, could easily have marked the end of Johnston's involvement with his alphabet.

LIVE ON THE HILLS
THE HIGHER UP THE FRESHER THE AIR

FROM APRIL
16 TH

THROUGH ELECTRIC TRAINS ELEPHANT & CASTLE AND WATFORD

4

Johnston Sans takes shape 1917–25

With war raging in Europe and Russia on the brink of revolution, movements in art and design were also edging towards a brave new world. Radical British thinkers like Frank Pick and other members of the Design and Industries Association (DIA) were absorbing ideas from the graphic design and architecture springing up across the Continent. So too were many of the Arts and Crafts community to which Johnston and Gill were affiliated.

The global conflict would have seemed far from rural Sussex, however, where it was very much business as usual. In 1916 Pepler moved into Gill's old Ditchling home and used his former workshop (previously a coaching house) as a site for a new printing press which became the focus of life in the village. Johnston, Gill and Pepler started a society that they named the Latin Club and for which Johnston handwrote a series of cards with an English word on one side and a Latin one on the reverse. They also began a little magazine in October 1916 called *The Game*, which was printed by Pepler with wood engravings by Gill and lettering by Johnston. Gill was becoming increasingly engrossed in the politics of

56 (opposite)

Produced by Charles Sharland in January 1917, this is thought to be the first colour poster using the Johnston Standard Alphabet, albeit with quite a free interpretation for the station names. It is also an excellent example of Pick's drive to increase passenger numbers by emulating the Metropolitan's successful 'Metro-land' campaign.

57

Two posters from 1916 using the new Johnston alphabet – tram fares (July) and an Arts and Crafts exhibition (November) – were harbingers of the century ahead, despite their somewhat plain appearance and lack of illustration. Undoubtedly an experiment, the one for tram fares even includes the first attempt at a white-out-of-black block. Spacing was narrowed, though too severely in places, on the exhibition poster.

the time, writing polemics and essays on the subject. Johnston moved to a small farm on Ditchling Common – which he bought in August 1916 after months trudging the Sussex lanes with Pepler looking for a suitable place. Hallets Farm was also very close to Hopkins Crank, Gill's house – and the three of them spent hours in each other's company discussing a wide range of topics, from politics to agriculture, and personal projects, such as Gill's at Westminster Abbey and Johnston's Underground alphabet.

Johnston's alphabet goes into production

Back at the UERL, as soon as Pick had approved Johnston's final submissions of June and July 1916, the next stage in the process of putting the alphabet into service was to make offset prints of the drawings, for which the letters had to be cut up and arranged in alphabetical order. One of the first posters made using the Johnston alphabet was a basic list of tram fares; another (serendipitously, given Johnston and Gill's creative interests) was for an Arts and Crafts Exhibition at the Royal Academy, which ran between October and December 1916 (fig.57). Here was the Johnston Standard Alphabet performing one of the jobs it was designed to do for London: a clear factual announcement of prices or events – unremarkable, yet honest, authoritative and practical. In both instances, the spacing – something Johnston had spent hours working on – was quite poorly executed, an issue that would be partially remedied, by the eventual cutting of the wooden type.

The UERL Mechanical Engineers Office meticulously redrew the letters and added handwritten instructions about how to reproduce them and scale them up or down. Waterlow and Sons were given the job of printing up what was known initially as the Standard Alphabet (to become Johnston Sans). Three separate double-crown sheets were made, two for the capitals and numerals – at two inches and 1⅓ inches – and a third for the lower case, at one inch. Five hundred copies of each set of lettering were then lithographically printed for sending out to printers and enamellers who were licensed to produce posters and signage for the Underground, as well as to any commercial artists (graphic designers) who might be commissioned to use it. Vehicle signwriters generally used the engineers' technical drawings (fig.60) to trace from, with the result that the sheets soon became worn, so the next step was to get the letters cut as wooden type. Rough

58

Trays of wooden Johnston type on view at the London Transport Museum Depot in Acton. The cutting of wooden type was not completed for Waterlow and Sons until 1921; the Underground Electric Railways of London's other favoured typefounder, Stephenson Blake, also had a set cut at around the same time.

59 (above left)

A rough pull from the first wooden type in 1917 labelled by Johnston as 'Final U.D. Alphabet'. The lithographically printed sheets of capitals were issued to printers in June as the 'Standard Alphabet' from which all other copying of the individual letters was to be done.

60 (above right)

Engineers' technical drawings (albeit versions from 1922, as none earlier are known to have survived) were used internally by signwriters. Progressively renamed 'Standard Alphabet' (here) and later 'Johnston Sans', these sheets are the basis for all facsimiles and revisions and have withstood a century of use and abuse.

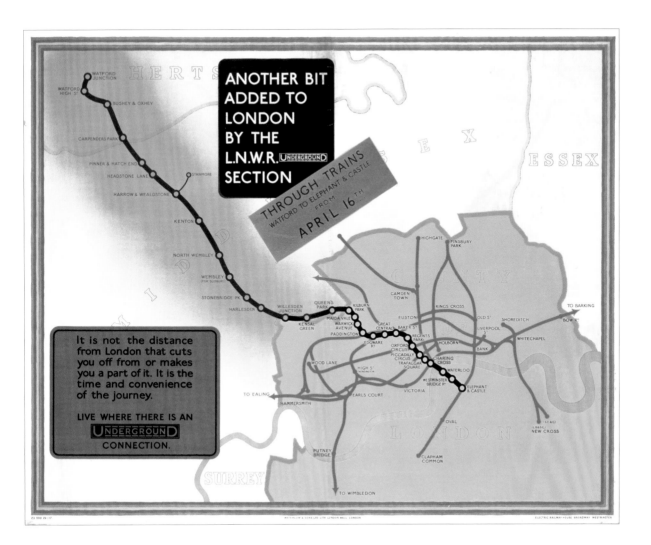

ANOTHER BIT
ADDED TO
LONDON
BY THE
L.N.W.R. UNDERGROUND
SECTION

THROUGH TRAINS
WATFORD TO ELEPHANT & CASTLE
FROM
APRIL 16TH

It is not the distance
from London that cuts
you off from or makes
you a part of it. It is the
time and convenience
of the journey.

LIVE WHERE THERE IS AN
UNDERGROUND
CONNECTION.

61
___

This poster from 1917 advertising the extension of the Bakerloo line to Watford (see also fig.56)
was among the first to incorporate Johnston's Standard Alphabet. All of the lettering was copied
by hand from the sheets of lettering printed at Waterlow's. Note the attempt to emulate
Johnston's lettering on the logo too.

pulls made at Waterlow's from the first blocks were sent to Johnston in May 1917 for his comments (fig.59). It was a time-consuming process, however, and the full complement of wooden type blocks was not completed until late 1921 (fig.58).

Aiming for the bull's-eye

It wasn't long before Pick had arranged for the Standard Alphabet letters to be used for the lettering on the Underground word itself. The large 'U and D' logotype set across a solid red disc had already been in place since 1912. Johnston was asked not just to add his lettering to the trademark (or logo as it would now be known) but to consider its overall design (see frontispiece). Johnston's response – probably based on the 'GENERAL' bar and circle, seen from around 1913 – was to hollow out the solid disc into a red ring. The 'UNDERGROUND' word in Johnston's alphabet, using slightly heavier letters, was delivered to Pick in May 1917. It included the dashes above and below the middle letters (which emulated the ceramic tile look from 1907–8), modified by Johnston with a triangular, chevron-like indentation at either end for a lighter effect. Sometimes referred to as 'ribbons', they echoed the diamond-shaped tittles above the 'i' and 'j'. 'London Memories', produced by the Avenue Press in 1918, were the first series of posters to use Johnston lettering on the logo (fig.62). They were followed in the same year by a series of information posters illustrated by cartoonist George Morrow (fig.63). These contained a lot more text, in both upper and lower case, plus the first public outing for the bar and ring device (all in red), known as the 'bull's-eye' (fig.63).

Johnston's new ring logo then appeared on a map cover in 1919. Still not quite satisfied with the spacing between the letters, Pick asked Johnston to take a look at it and to consider re-proportioning the whole logo at the same time. The revised logo, worked on by Johnston in 1919–20, was neater and better balanced (the larger 'U and D' now coinciding with the border of the outer edge of the ring). It appeared on the map cover from 1921 onwards. In the meantime, Johnston was working on revised logos for the rest of the UERL empire. The Tramways one was completed in 1920, along with one for General buses.

A squeeze on the buses

UERL omnibuses, run under the banner of 'General', had long been a source of concern for Pick as their destination board letters could be difficult to decipher

64 (above)

Johnston's Omnibus Type for the K-Type bus was painted on to destination boards, as on the Number 11 route shown, but some of the handiwork was a bit hit and miss. At the same time, he also redesigned the General bus logo using an even heavier letterform than his Underground one.

65 (above right)

Although the condensed letters on the destination board of this B-Type bus from 1916 were not as bad as some, they were still a little too condensed – something Johnston tried to improve upon.

as the bus approached (fig.65). Johnston's solution was a condensed form of the Underground lettering he called Omnibus Type (fig.64). His first rough sketch was presented to Pick in December 1919, but as it did not conform with police regulations for size and legibility, Johnston was permitted to use abbreviations to fit the restricted space on destination boards. In January 1920, Johnston began working in earnest on three-inch-high condensed capitals for a destination board for an imaginary bus journey whose route would take it over Richmond and Kew Bridges to Turnham Green and down Hammersmith Broadway: an awkward combination of long names and difficult letters.[1] To fit the board the letter 'O' was squeezed into almost half the width of the original 'O', and by a clever trick of raising the bowl of the 'P' and 'R', Johnston was able to preserve some of its roundness. The final alphabet was delivered in April 1920, and a set of numerals 6½ inches high was ready by early May.

A unified look for station signage

There is some speculation that the Standard Alphabet was not necessarily envisaged as being designed for the entire range of UERL lettering, the signage included. But this seems a bit nonsensical, as Pick had stated that he wanted the lettering to look clear on flat surfaces, which presumably would apply not just to paper. In addition, it is known that he was searching for a style of lettering that would give a unified look to all UERL signage and printed material, and was

especially keen to avoid the visual incoherence of a system formed by adding new elements in a piecemeal fashion. Consequently, the Standard Alphabet very quickly migrated to signage.

It would not have been economical to replace every expensive enamel sign with an identical one set in the Standard Alphabet, but whenever a new sign was needed, it made sense to switch to one in the Johnston typeface. When new Underground extensions were built from the 1920s onwards, almost every sign was manufactured using the Johnston lettering. Once the transition had been made, it was virtually unheard of for any sign or lettering made for the UERL network not to feature the Standard Alphabet (or at least an attempt to look like it). This was an incredible feat of typographical unification for any organisation, even by modern standards.

In the early 1920s, when the Charing Cross, Euston & Hampstead Railway (known later as the Northern line) was being extended from Golders Green to Edgware, Pick and his architect, Stanley Heaps (1880–1962), chose to incorporate the Johnston lettering into the designs from the outset (fig.67). Changes were also needed to some of the existing stations and here, too, the new alphabet was employed (fig.66). Planning was now under way for a southerly extension, and here architect Charles Holden (1875–1960) was commissioned for all the stations down to Morden. Holden, also influenced by Arts and Crafts and an admirer of Johnston, embraced the new Underground bar and circle logo and lettering, building the bull's-eye into station fronts as an architectural centrepiece.

Keeping it in the UERL family

Pick always felt that the lettering he had commissioned from Johnston should stay within the confines of the UERL. This was a wise move: how easy it would have

66 (above left)

Where improvements were required further down the City & South London Railway, such as here at Borough, photographed in 1922, the new lettering was applied to station name signs (but not the 'WAY OUT' ones).

67 (above right)

Brent station photographed in September 1923 two months before its opening while the finishing touches were still being added. The name on the architrave is in relief Johnston, and by November the station name sign sported the lettering too. With Hendon Central, this was one of the first stations to open along the extension to what became the Northern line.

BRITISH EMPIRE EXHIBITION

68 (above)

Promotional material for the British Empire Exhibition held at Wembley Park included some lettering that resembled Johnston's petits-serifs (p.59).

69 (above right)

Poster designers were quick to use artistic licence on Johnston's lettering. Here a detail from Charles Shepard's 1924 promotion of the Edgware extension.

70 (opposite)

A 1925 travel poster, typical of others from the period. Though the 'Norfolk Broads' letters are slightly expanded, the 'LNER' initials, especially those on the left-hand side, seem to hint at things to come.

been for printers to allow the lettering to be used for a trade advertisement that might appear on an Underground platform and be possibly mistaken for an official notice. And so the alphabet remained the intellectual property, as it would now be termed, of London Transport and its descendants. However, there have been a few instances over the years where it has slipped out of its protected domain. One of the earliest cases was the 1924 British Empire Exhibition. The event was such a vast undertaking, with so much promotional material, that many typefaces were associated with it, but several official publications featured Johnston-esque letterforms (fig.68). In those non-litigious days, no court cases were filed, but it shows the growing influence of the Johnston lettering.

The four big national railway companies all had their terminals in London, hence none of them were immune to the impact that Pick, Holden and Johnston's work was having on the image of transport, especially in the form of promotional material. One of the sharpest operators was the London & North Eastern Railway (LNER), under the leadership of district passenger manager Cecil Dandridge. From as far back as 1924, LNER posters show tentative moves towards embracing a sans serif. An examination of material uncovered by Beverley Cole and Richard Durack reveals that lettering used in the mid 1920s, pre-dating Gill's 1926 lettering for a bookshop (p.82), partly bridges the gap between Johnston and Gill (fig.70).[2]

Letters in the hills

Although Gill was briefly pulled into the orbit of the British Empire Exhibition, in terms of lettering the early 1920s were dominated by Johnston. Having

L·N·E·R

V·L·DANVERS

NORFOLK
BROADS
BY L·N·E·R

71

The Empire Marketing Board (1926–33)
used the actual Johnston lettering in the
mid–late 1920s.

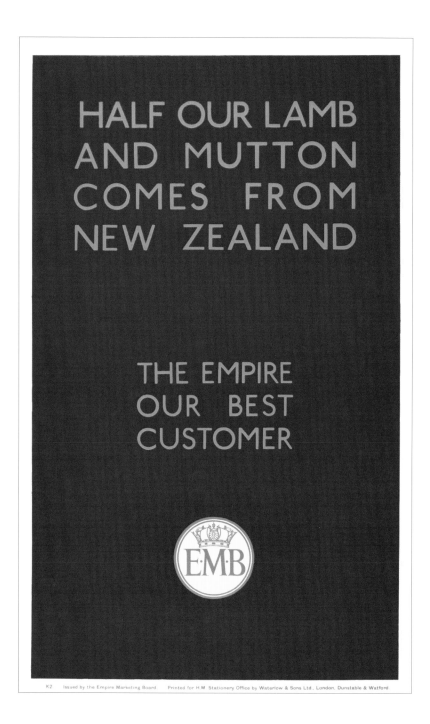

completed his *Stations of the Cross*, Gill was engaged in many other sculpting projects, plus some commissions for the Royal Mint. He made a design for the florin, half-crown and the crown in 1924 and proofs were made for his threepence, sixpence and one-shilling coins the following year. He also worked on a proposed design for the one-pound note. None of these designs were produced, however. By 1924 Gill had tired of Ditchling and was searching for a more remote location in which to live and work. Quite suddenly, he upped sticks and moved to an abandoned former monastery at Capel-y-ffin in the Black Mountains on the Welsh borders, meaning that his close personal and working relationship with Johnston – tested earlier when Gill converted to Catholicism while Johnston remained staunchly Anglican[3] – was severely diminished, although the pair did stay in touch.

Despite its remoteness, Gill's new Welsh home attracted many visitors, including long-term supporter Harry Kessler, who arrived in January 1925. To help guide his visitors around the village, Gill created what Fiona MacCarthy describes as a 'sans serif for various handpainted notices round Capel, most noticeably the MEN and WOMEN signs made for the chapel to show which sex stood where'.[4] In a letter to his brother Evan, Gill described notices painted by Laurence, the brother of Gill's assistant Joseph Cribb, on signposts leading up from the nearest railway station in Gill's early sans serif, offering such way-finding guidance as 'THIS WAY TO THE CHURCH'.[5]

None of these makeshift signs are known to have survived, but an insight into the direction that Gill's work was taking can perhaps be gleaned from other projects of this period. For example, it is understood to be Gill who drew some letters for an advertisement for W. G. Briggs & Co. of Chancery Lane in 1924, possibly one of his earliest attempts to form a sans serif style of lettering (fig.73). Gill wrote during this time that he had made experiments with block letters on advertisements (including some for Selfridges' stores), which would seem to back this up, though none of these remain on record. There is also a reference to a contract in a letter of May 1925 from Gill to his friend Desmond Chute:

> I'm doing a set of alphabets for the Army & Navy Stores for all their
> notices and signs: this is an interesting job for it is: 1, how I do good

Stanley Morison

William Rothenstein's sketch of Stanley Morison as it appeared in Lanston Monotype Corporation's in-house publication, the *Monotype Recorder*.

Essex-born Stanley Morison (1889–1967) was as much of a devotee of the Arts and Crafts movement as Johnston and Gill. In 1913 he was briefly editorial assistant for *The Imprint* (p.47) but, as a conscientious objector, he was incarcerated at the start of the war. After his release at the end of hostilities, he joined the Pelican Press and in 1922 became a founder member of the typographic Fleuron Society with Meynell, Holbrook Jackson, Bernard Newdigate and Oliver Simon, editing three editions of the society's journal, *The Fleuron*, between 1925 and 1930. He also edited the *Penrose Annual* (published 1895–1982) between 1923 and 1925. From 1923 Morison became an adviser on type design to the Lanston Monotype Corporation.

One of his first tasks was to adapt several typefaces for the Monotype casting system, including a classic serif typeface revival in the English style based on the type designed by John Baskerville (1757), which was used on the company's machines in 1923, followed by his adapted version of Bembo, another serif in 1929, based on one of the earliest roman typefaces cut by Francesco Griffo for Venetian printer Aldus Manutius in 1495. Aside from his association with Gill (p.86), he also played a leading role in typographic thought and criticism, publishing a number of books and papers on the subject. Published in 1936, his *First Principles of Typography* deals at length with such issues as leading, white space and the setting out of index and contents pages. Morison publicly criticised the lettering used in *The Times* newspaper, which led to him being engaged to create a new typeface for the paper. Working alongside Victor Lardent, he produced Times New Roman, first used in 1932 (although there is some controversy about the origins of it).[7]

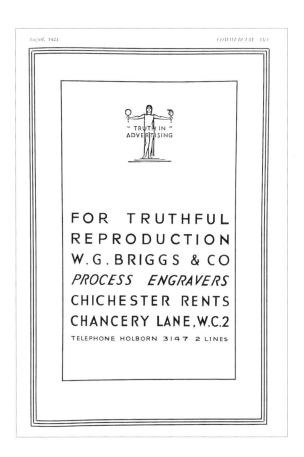

letters; 2, absolutely legible-to-the-last-degree letters; 3, letters which any fool can copy accurately and easily. So I'm doing them simple block letters. It's rather fun cutting great big letters out of white paper and sticking them on big black sheets – they don't half stare at you – fine test for astigmatism . . .[6]

Sadly none of this lettering is known to have survived either.

It was during 1925 that influential typographer Stanley Morison first began working with Gill. They had known each other as far back as 1913, when Morison wrote for *The Imprint* but by the mid 1920s, Morison was advising the Lanston Monotype Corporation on type design. Gill was tasked with developing a new serif typeface that came to be known as Perpetua. But that work was somewhat overshadowed by what was to prove to be Gill's greatest achievement.

73

The cover of the August 1924 edition of *Commercial Art*, attributed to 'Gill', with a display advertisement for W. G. Briggs & Co. inside the magazine. While it is not known if the cover was by Gill, even though it is loosely in his style, the advertisement is believed to be by him. Possibly an early experiment by Gill in sans serif lettering, it is a very mixed bunch – notice the 'R' and 'S' have at least three variants.

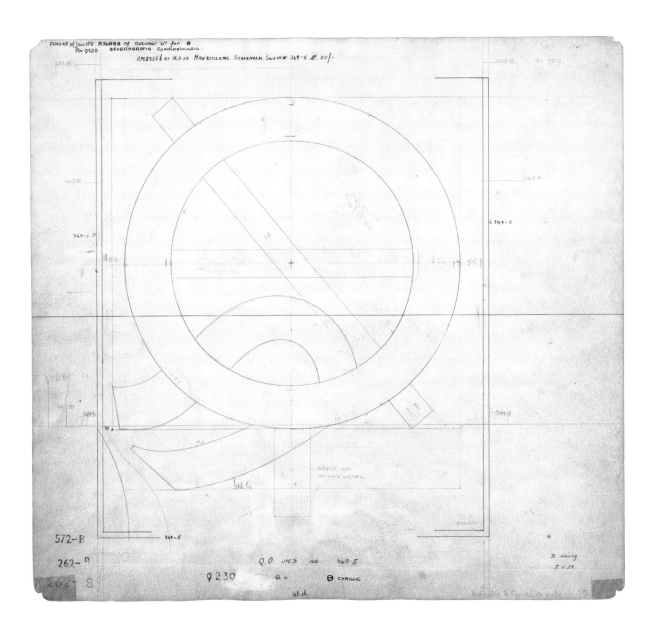

FH4048 of Jan 1971 R36888 of October '67 for θ
for Q230   SEVEROGRAFIA Czechoslovakia.
CM23556 of 18.3.50 MAURITZONS. STOCKHOLM. SWEDEN. 349-5 Å. 25/-

262-6   262-B   B. 928

262-B   262-P

349-6 >   < 349-5

56   55

572-B   349-5

262-B   3475

91 >

                              13

                    STUCK ON
                    IN HOT METAL

std Q

572-B   349-5

262-P   Q.O USED for 349-5   D. Laing
                                                                 7.11.29.

262-8 8   Q 230   Q 91   θ CYRILLIC

                              std   Available to Cyrillic (2) only

5

Gill's fascia to face 1926–32

The mid 1920s was an incredibly fertile period for art and design: the Bauhaus, art deco and surrealism were all in full swing and a new breed of European typographers was developing geometric alphabets like Erbar (p.29), Kabel and Futura (p.122). Although British graphic designers were keeping up with the times, this had yet to percolate down to the type founders.

Gill's nearest large city – or the one that he chose to frequent during his years in Wales – was Bristol, where his friend and former life-drawing model Douglas Cleverdon lived. During the summer of 1926, Cleverdon opened a bookshop just off Park Street in the Clifton area of the city. Soon to become the haunt of artists and intellectuals, it was a haven for Gill. Knowing about Gill's previous lettering commissions for shopfronts, Cleverdon asked his friend that autumn if he would paint the signboard to go above the window. It turned out to be one of the most fortuitous projects he had ever undertaken; indeed, serendipity seems to have played a part in many of Gill's commissions. Cleverdon describes

74 (opposite)

A Monotype production drawing, ten inches high, for the capital 'Q' of Gill Sans in the 262 Series. Signed by 'D. Laing', it would have been generated using Monotype's 'magic lantern' projection system (p.88). In later years the drawing was added to: in 1950 for Swedish and in October 1967 for Czechoslovakian variants.

This now quite famous photo (the only one known to exist) of the fascia painted by Gill for Douglas Cleverdon's Bristol bookshop in October 1926 was admired by Morison when he visited (March 1927) and it was the inspiration for what became Gill Sans.

how, despite suffering from a bout of flu, Gill, not to be deterred, lay in bed 'delineating a couple of alphabets in Roman and sans serif which I could use as models for notices in the bookshop'.[1] Gill readily admits that they and his future typeface were loosely based on the work he had discussed with Johnston,[2] along with the Capel-y-ffin notices painted by Cribb (p.77). Over the next two days, 31 October to 1 November 1926, on a long white wooden board, Gill then painted two simple words, 'DOUGLAS CLEVERDON' (fig.75), using the sans serif letters he had just sketched. Cleverdon used Gill's book of pencil-written alphabets for tracing the lettering to make signs for inside the shop (fig.76). As the *Monotype Recorder* remarked some years later:

> the pencilled letter forms are not of course designs for type; they are models for the guidance of amateur letterers. But the juxtaposition of normal and monotone forms would alone indicate that Eric Gill was putting

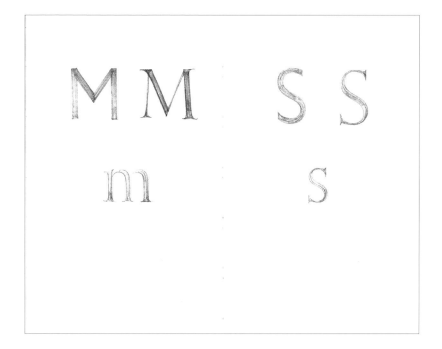

76

Pages from a notebook produced for lettering and signs around Cleverdon's shop were later printed by his bookpress as *A Book of Alphabets for Douglas Cleverdon*, reissued in 1987 as a limited edition by Gill's nephew Christopher Skelton. Revealingly, Gill called these early forays his 'block letter', harking back to the discussions with Pick, Meynell and Johnston (p.55).

the leisure of those days of convalescence to a comparative study which would confirm in his own mind principles of aptness, fitness-for-purpose, that underlie all sound arguments about type design.[3]

Gill's notebook, *A Book of Alphabets,* dated 30 October 1926 (fig.76), shows such confidence and clarity of thought on what a block letter should be that it is worth any student of design tracking it down. In common with Johnston's work, Gill's 'A', 'M' and 'N' have squared-off, as opposed to pointy, tops. But his 'W' and 'V' differ slightly from Johnston's, with pointed bottoms. In common with Johnston's, Gill's middle section of the 'M' does not touch the baseline (a clever trick to avoid the space it occupies being too wide, which looks odd when set with other letters). Both Johnston's and Gill's 'C', 'D', 'G' and 'Q' are based on the entirely circular 'O'. A decade after Johnston, Gill's 'Q' is given a more extravagant calligraphic tail. As with Johnston, the 'C' and 'G' both feature a sheared terminal (as if the rest of a circle has been lopped right off), but Johnston's unique 'S' was avoided by Gill, who chose to shear the terminals to match the 'C' and 'G' (making it one of his most defining letters). The horizontal bar of Gill's 'E' and 'F', unlike Johnston's, match the top one. His initial 'J' was a work in progress and early sketches show a most flourishing calligraphic terminal, later revised by Monotype into a sheared end. Gill's most

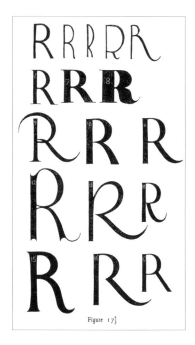

Figure 17}

distinctive letter was his 'R': it is given an elegantly curved tail (fig.77). Mosley calls it Gill's 'Florentine R' with a 'sprung tail' after Roman inscriptions in stone.[4]

Holden's bold new look

As well as being pivotal for Gill, 1926 was a big year for the Underground too, and hence for Johnston. The long-awaited southerly extension to Morden (which become the Northern line) opened in September. A large number of posters and information leaflets were created in the Johnston alphabet (fig.79). This was to encourage passengers to use the trains, partly because Morden itself was relatively unpopulated and the UERL needed to run bus services to it from neighbouring areas like Sutton (which the extension was originally intended to serve) in order to fill up the trains. Charles Holden's radical entrances for the stations along the new line featured large glass panels that encompassed the bull's-eye logo and featured Johnston's Standard Alphabet on blue enamelled panels (fig.78). The simplicity and clarity of these pleased Pick so much that he employed Holden for the reconstruction of Piccadilly Circus and commissioned from him designs for the new headquarters of the Underground

77 (above)

Gill's *Essay on Typography* includes this illustration of his views on different 'R's, some of which he describes as 'pure fancifulness'.

78 (right)

Balham station opened in the mid 1920s (seen here in a later photograph). The southerly extension to Morden was an opportunity for the architect Holden to build the stations as a unified piece of design, creating some of London's most modern and radical-looking architecture but which have stood the test of time.

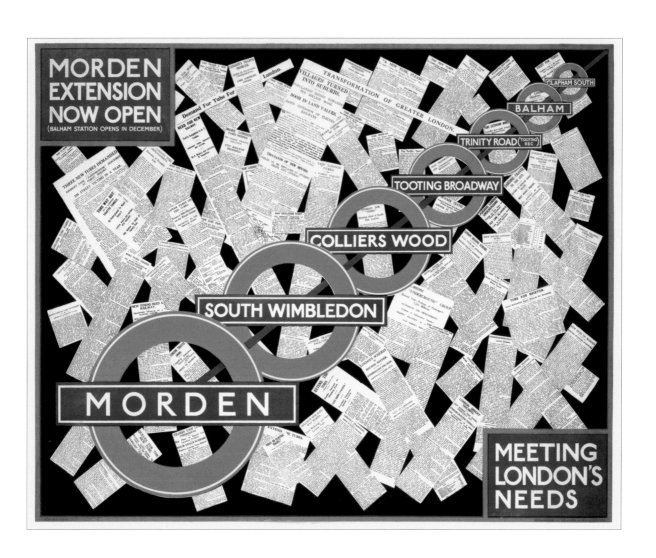

79

A poster from 1926 displays the impact of
Johnston's letters and his bar and ring device.

80 (opposite)

Gill's early sketches for Monotype, 6 June 1927 (top), in Indian ink on thin brown paper (rather than graph paper, as they would be later). Produced just nine months after the Cleverdon alphabet book, these letters are very similar in style. By February 1928, Gill was already working out more detailed comparisons of the letters and their relation to each other. A sketch from 19 March 1928 shows the numerals (bottom right). Gill's choice of letters from his own name (bottom left) is not entirely egotistical: his detailed study of 'E', 'R' and 'L' also indicates how the 'G' differs from the 'C'.

at 55 Broadway. Rather than use Johnston's lettering for signage here, though, Pick commissioned a new designer, Percy John Delf Smith – albeit from the same typographical 'stable', as he was a former student of Johnston (p.99).

Gill's sans shows its face

Far from the rarified world of display lettering, Monotype was developing the Super Caster. Released in 1928 and especially designed for setting headlines, rather than body text, it was one of the most advanced forms of typesetting of its day. As the company's adviser on type design, Morison realised that something different would be needed for the new machine. Responsible for adapting classic serif faces for Monotype (p.78), he was also aware of the growing popularity of modern sans serifs, especially on the Continent. It was at this time, in March 1927, that Morison made a chance visit to Bristol, happening to call in at the Cleverdon bookshop, where he caught sight of Gill's lettering (fig.75). It was a pivotal moment in typographic history. He advised Monotype that they should commission a set of sans serif titling capitals from Gill, while Perpetua (which Gill had already been commissioned to produce for them) was still being prepared for distribution. Gill was given a salary by Monotype and began sketches for his sans as early as June 1927 (fig.80). Basing his new letters on those in the Cleverdon alphabet book, Gill produced an impressive array of hand-inked drawings over the next few months, demonstrating both his élan and precision as a designer. Many of the letters were altered by him (in white paint) either to meet the requirements of Monotype or due to his own fastidiousness.

According to print historian Sebastian Carter, staff at Monotype's type-drawing office were somewhat sceptical at first. Frank Hinman Pierpont, Monotype's foundry manager, is reported to have said: 'I can see nothing in this design to recommend it and much that is objectionable.'[5] The department did a lot of work during late 1927 to make Gill's drawings fit the exacting specifications of the machine processes. To help with the fine-tuning, Gill's hand-drawn letters were each loaded into a 'magic lantern', which then projected a magnified image onto vertical board so that, using the larger images, technicians could make more accurate versions of each letter (fig.81). Robin Nicholas, employed decades later (1965) at Monotype, explained how the device worked: 'It was a kind of horizontal microscope that enlarged the two-inch drawings via lenses

ABCDEFGH
IJKLMNQRS
TUWXYZ

EG 652

231 — 24 Title

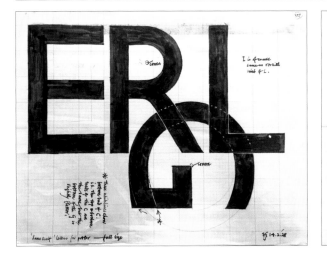

ERL
G

I is drawn same as vertical with 4 L.

* These initials are drawn letters bold + C.
is the top of bottoms
with the C and
the lower part the
bottom - this G is
slightly flatter.

Same serif letters for poster — full size

EG 14.2.28

1 2 3 3 4 5
6 7 8 9 o

*note: for a larger weight
width O from
the alphabet*

EG 19.3.28

A letter 'M' projected by 'magic lantern' for further adjustment by Monotype. Enlarged to ten inches in height, the letter was then traced (as here) in order to smooth out any inaccuracies, then copied by pantograph at a reduced scale onto a wax-coated plate.

so they could be traced and fine-tuned before being reduced precisely to the right point size.'[6] It was on 14 January 1928 that the first pulls from the Super Caster of what was temporarily termed Morison Gill Face were reported to have been made.

Four months later, in May 1928, the titling capitals were displayed for the first time at a trade exhibition for the annual meeting of the Federation of Master Printers in Blackpool. Morison made a presentation entitled 'Robbing the Printer' to the delegates, pointing out that advertising and publicity agents were more in touch with modern design than they were. The cover for the exhibition's programme, headed 'Publicity and Selling Congress' (fig.82), provided the first outing for the new typeface, now known inside the company as 'New Sans'. According to Christopher Skelton, however, 'Gill's designs did not meet with universal approval and Morison [reported] that "an insolent and truculent section" of the Master Printers had described them as "typographical bolshevism"'.[7] This was not the kind of welcome Monotype had hoped for, but help was at hand in the form of one Paul Beaujon, an influential typeface critic whom the corporation had hired, and who, somewhat to its surprise, turned out to be not an elderly Frenchman but the *nom de plume* of Beatrice Warde, a young American woman in her mid twenties. Writing articles praising Gill in the *Monotype Recorder* and *The Fleuron*, Warde enthusiastically assisted in the marketing of Gill Sans. A relationship with Morison and a brief fling with Gill may have helped, but her promotion of the new typeface was undoubtedly genuine because she approved so wholeheartedly of Gill's designs.

ANNUAL ✳ MEETING ¶ FEDERATION OF MASTER PRINTERS

BLACKPOOL

PUBLICITY AND
SELLING CONGRESS

on Monday, 21st May, 1928

at the Imperial Hydro Hotel

at 2.30 p.m.

¶ ANNUAL MEETING

FEDERATION
OF
MASTER
PRINTERS

THE LANSTON MONOTYPE CORPORATION LIMITED, LONDON
PRESENT
AN INTERIM PROOF OF THEIR
SANS-SERIF TITLING
DESIGNED BY ERIC GILL

CONGRESS
SELLING
AND
PUBLICITY

BLACKPOOL

GILL SANS SERIF
A BRILLIANT LETTER
CUT BY A FAMOUS SCULPTOR
RANGING FROM 14 TO 36 POINT
ABCDEFGHIJKLMNOPQRSTUVWXYZ

82 (above)

The programme cover and type specimen for Morison's talk to the Federation of Master Printers, 21 May 1928, marked the first appearance in print of Gill's new lettering. The leaflet specified that the 'Sans-Serif Titling', in series 231, was available in five sizes.

83

Promotional advert for the typeface here called 'Gill Sans Serif' displayed in the *Monotype Recorder*, July 1928.

84 (opposite)

During the summer of 1928, Gill was working on drawings for other weights of his new typeface. Dated 15 July, the sketch on the left, for some lower-case letters, was enlarged to embrace the full alphabet five days later (bottom). The sketch from 8 August 1928 (top right) shows how Gill believed the lower case would sit with his capitals. As Monotype had by then decided to retain the titling capitals as their own self-standing series (231), however, a new catalogue number (262) was issued for Gill's revised caps and lower case.

85 (right)

The July 1928 edition (no.226) of the *Monotype Recorder*, an 'Advertising Number', the cover shown here, was devoted to promoting 'Gill Sans Titling Series 231'.

THE MONOTYPE RECORDER
Special Articles in this Number
"THE ADVERTISER AND HIS PRINTER"
By H. J. B. Morris
WHAT MUST THE PRINTER KNOW ABOUT ADVERTISING?
By A. Philip Henderson
"TELLING THE BUYER OF PRINTING"
—and several practical articles on the Advertising of Printing, with many illustrations

A D V E R T I S I N G

Now in Press
"THE ADVERTEASER"
a burlesque "Daily," with many small advertisements to demonstrate the pulling power of "Monotype" publicity faces. For a good laugh— and some new layout hints—send in the enclosed card for your free copy!

86 (left)

A sketch (far left) from 24 July showing Gill's first foray into italics, known simply as 'Gill Sans'. This was followed by a sketch for the lower-case italics (left).

Inked drawings of Gill's bold lettering from February 1929. He was working on this weight up until 1931.

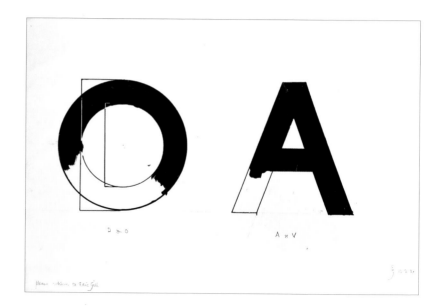

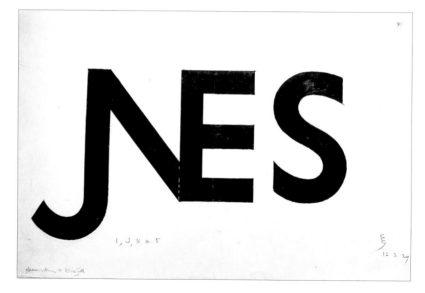

A buyer . . .

The first major take-up of Gill Sans by a large industrial user was in 1929 when Cecil Dandridge, the LNER's advertising manager, chose it as the in-house typeface following a conversation with Gill the previous year. Winning the LNER over was a huge boost for Monotype because the railway company was such a prolific commissioner of every kind of printed material, from timetables to illustrated colour posters, using the services of up to 90 different printers to churn out around 40 million items a year. Each of these printing houses was now required to order Gill Sans from Monotype as part of what became known as the 'LNER Standardisation'.[8] The LNER, having adopted the style for their in-house lettering, then applied it universally, from railway timetables to engine nameplates. Swapping over to the new typeface and revised designs for the hundreds of timetables and circulars was not a rapid task; it took until 1932 for the LNER's own massive print works in Stratford, east London, to be fully equipped with the new type, for instance. Echoing an early application of the first printed sans serif, Gill Sans was employed for a timetable (fig.89). Its first appearance in a newspaper advertisement was for *The Times* (12 March 1929, fig.90) for an exhibition of LNER posters, followed later that month by an advertisement for holidays on the East Coast (this one incorporating an additional few lines of Blado italic).

. . . and a competitor

In 1928, with Johnston's letters splashed across London, Gill Sans beginning to make its presence felt and German typographers rattling off new sans serifs like they were going out of fashion, a respected British printing firm called the Curwen Press issued a supplement to their own type-specimen book. First

88

A Monotype brochure from 1929 illustrates the first three weights of Gill's lettering available: titling capitals (series 231); the regular 'Gill Sans u. & l.c.' (series 262); and the 'Gill Bold' (275), consisting only of caps at this stage.

Timetable (a.m. columns, with "From Baldock" shown at right):

#	Station														From Baldock
1	HITCHIN ... dep.														7 52
2	Stevenage														8 0
3	Knebworth														8 7
4	Welwyn North														8 14
5	Welwyn Garden City ... arr.														8 18
6	Hatfield ... arr. / dep.					8 6 / 8 11									
8	Brookman's Park					8 12									
9	Potters Bar and South Mimms					8 18									
10	Hadley Wood					8 23									
11	New Barnet			8 14		8 27									
12	Oakleigh Park for East Barnet			8 16					8 21						
13	New Southgate and Friern Barnet			8 22					8 23						
14	Wood Green (Alexandra Park) ... arr.			8 25					8 28						
15	Wood Green (Alexandra Park) ... dep.	8 27		8 27		8 30			8 32						
16	Hornsey			8 30							8 38	8 38	8 38		8 42
17	Harringay			8 33					8 37			8 41			8 45
18	HIGH BARNET	8 7							8 18						
19	Totteridge and Whetstone	8 11							8 22						
20	Woodside Park for Nth. Finchley	8 14							8 25						
21	Finchley (Church End) ... arr.	8 17							8 28						
22	Finchley (Church End) ... dep.	8 18							8 30						
23	East Finchley	8 22													
24	ALEXANDRA PALACE				8 20		8 24						8 32		
25	Muswell Hill				8 22		8 26						8 34		
26	Cranley Gardens				8 25		8 29						8 37		
27	Highgate		8 27		8 28		8 32						8 40		
28	Crouch End				8 31		8 35			8 38			8 43		
29	Stroud Green				8 33		8 37			8 40			8 45		
30	FINSBURY PARK ... arr. / dep.	8 32 / 8 34	8 35 / 8 37	8 36		8 38 / 8 40			8 39 / 8 41	8 42 / 8 44	8 43 / 8 44	8 45		8 47 / 8 49
32	Canonbury		8 41						8 48						
33	Mildmay Park		8 43						8 50						
34	Dalston Junction		8 45						8 52						
35	Haggerston		8 50												
36	Shoreditch		8 49												
37	BROAD STREET ... arr.		8 52												
38	York Road (King's Cross) ... dep.		8 40				8 48			8 54					
39	KING'S CROSS (Terminus) ... arr.	8 38				8 42 8 46		8 48		8 50		8 52		8 56
40	King's Cross (Metropolitan) ... dep.		8 43				8 51			8 57					
41	Farringdon and High Holborn		8 47				8 55			9 1					
42	Aldersgate and Barbican		8 49				8 57			9 3					
43	MOORGATE STREET ... arr.		8 51				8 59			9 5					

A Passengers for Haggerston change at Dalston Junction

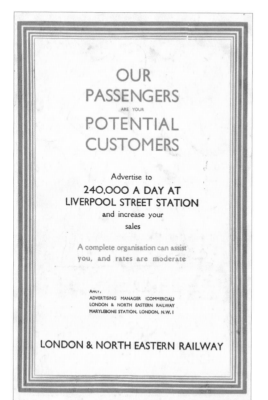

L.N.E.R.
MONOTYPE GILL SANS SERIF.

Specimens of characters, figures, &c., standardised for the L.&N.E.R. All types used must conform in outline and weight with these specimens.

ABCDEFGHIJKLMNOPQRSTUVWXYZ&ÆŒ
abcdefghijklmnopqrstuvwxyzæœfifflflfiffl
£$1234567890   ..,.;:-"'!?()[]—

ABCDEFGHIJKLMNOPQRSTUVWXYZ&ÆŒ
abcdefghijklmnopqrstuvwxyzæœfifflflfiffl
£1234567890   ..,.;:-"'!?()[]†§

ABCDEFGHIJKLMNOPQRSTUVWXYZ&ÆŒ
abcdefghijklmnopqrstuvwxyzæœfifflflfiffl   £$1234567890   ..,.;:-"'!?()[]—

ABCDEFGHIJKLMNOPQRSTUVWXYZ&ÆŒ
abcdefghijklmnopqrstuvwxyzæœfifflflfiffl
£$1234567890   ..,.;:-"'!?()[]—

ABCDEFGHIJKLMNOPQRSTUVWXYZ&ÆŒ
abcdefghijklmnopqrstuvwxyzfiflfffffiffl
£1234567890   ..,.;:-"'-!?[]()§†

ABCDEFGHIJKLMNOPQRSTUVWXYZ
abcdefghijklmnopqrstuvwxyzæœfifflflfiffl
£$1234567890   ..,.;:-"'!?()[]—   &ÆŒ

established in 1863, at Plaistow in east London, by 1911 it had come under the management of Harold Curwen, the founder's grandson. Having become involved with the Design and Industries Association (DIA), along with Pick and others, and, crucially, having been one of Johnston's lettering students, Curwen was gaining a reputation for extremely high-quality material. As well as employing its own craftspeople and designers, the press commissioned work from foremost artists of the day, including Edward Bawden (1903–89), Paul Nash (1889–1946), Edward McKnight Kauffer (1899–1954) and Eric Ravilious (1903–42).

Undoubtedly a talented typographer in his own right, Curwen had designed his own sans serif. As a type-specimen supplement proclaims: 'This series is based on an alphabet designed in 1912 by Harold Curwen. It was revised and cut as type in 1928'[9] (fig.93). Whether Curwen's sans serif pre-dates Johnston and Gill, there is no reason to suppose that Curwen's claim is untrue, but as Justin Howes has discovered, while some letters may have been created by Curwen for West Ham Corporation tramcars from 1912, the full upper-case alphabet did not appear until 1924.[10] Either way, it raises a number of questions. To start with, no drawings appear to have survived from 1912. At this time Curwen was undoubtedly within the orbit of Johnston, Gill and the Lincoln's Inn crowd. Had he ever shown his ideas for a block letter to them, and what did they think of it, if so? The year 1912 was of course a good three years before Pick commissioned Johnston and Gill to design an alphabet for the Underground. Might Pick have seen Curwen's work then, and been influenced by it? Why did Curwen wait until 1928 to cut his own type, and did he ever discuss his lettering with Johnston or Gill? Did he start working on the type cutting before or at the same time as Gill was working on his?

Unfortunately, there are no clear responses to any of these questions and they remain tantalisingly unanswered for the most part. What is clear, however, is that the power and beauty of Curwen Sans capitals have meant that they have endured. Often substituted for Johnston (and Gill) by printers who did not have the originals or the right sizes or, on occasion, deliberately used from the outset, this typeface proved a competent and aesthetically pleasing alternative for either. It is worth noting one example of Curwen Sans in existence before Gills Sans: an Essex window-making company called Crittall used the Curwen letters in the early 1920s as printed line-blocks but, after a while, probably for reasons of economy, had them made into type by Curwen (fig.94). Crittall

89 (top left)

A timetable that Monotype claims to be the first set in Gill Sans for the London and North Eastern Railway (LNER).

90 (top right)

One of the earliest appearances of Gill Sans Titling in a newspaper advert, this appeared on 12 March 1929 in *The Times*. Later that month the LNER began promoting the *Holiday Handbook* in advertisements that also used Gill Sans.

91 (bottom left)

The new sans serif was soon seen on all LNER literature, such as this 1930 press call for other advertisers.

92 (bottom right)

The company called its version of the typeface 'LNER Monotype Gill Sans Serif'.

93 (right)

Claimed by its designer Harold Curwen
to have been based on letters he drew in
1912, this stylish sans serif was not cut as
metal type until 1928.

94 (far right)

The only known use of Curwen before
1928 was as line blocks created for
window-manufacturer Crittall. This
lettering from their 1928 catalogue cover,
though with some differences to the type,
does seem to indicate Curwen's work.

installed glass at the Bauhaus in Germany, the Hoover Building in London and
some of Holden's Underground stations, so clearly had a good eye for design.

Johnston emboldened

With the exception of a few minor revisions and improvements to his original
typeface – which went on until about 1940 – Johnston had now returned
almost entirely to his pen-and-ink lettering, moving in the mid 1920s from his
'Foundational' to his more 'Gothic Compressed' hand. But the range of the
initial Underground typeface was proving limiting and Pick wanted to develop a
heavier version. The Standard Alphabet of 1916 was much less heavy than some
of the other sans serifs in circulation at that time, leading to calls by printers
for something with greater weight, particularly for use in larger display items.
Some had followed Johnston's own lead, copying the slight emboldening of the
letters used in the bar and circle logos (especially the 'GENERAL' bus one, see
frontispiece) to create their own bolder forms.

The UERL was highly conscious of the arrival of Monotype's Gill Sans and
the impact that it might have on their publicity. Howes quotes a comment from
Pick on the subject in 1930:

95 (opposite)

The lettering on this 1926 Metropolitan
poster by 'SHEP' foreshadows Percy Delf
Smith's Dorno with petits-serifs.

SHEP

SPEND A DAY IN
METRO-LAND

GORGEOUS AUTUMNAL SCENERY
CHARMING COUNTRY WALKS

GET A COPY OF "METRO-LAND" AT ANY BOOKING OFFICE OR BOOKSTALL
PRICE TWOPENCE

R·H·SELBIE GENERAL MANAGER
BAKER STREET STATION N·W·I

G.1848/990   SANDERS PHILLIPS & CO., LTD., Chryssell Road, London, S.W.9

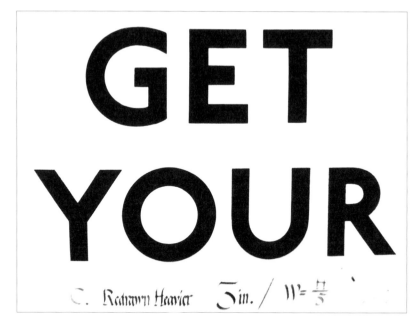

With this type at their disposal many advertisers may produce bills which are somewhat like our own. This makes all the more urgent our plan to secure from Johnston further designs for letters of a larger scale with conventional type ornaments, so that we may enrich our bills and keep them distinctive.[11]

The UERL's own technical department had also jumped the gun and prepared transfer letters that were considerably bolder than Johnston's original submissions (fig.96). Johnston had always told his students that there was only a certain elasticity in emboldening letters until they became useless. Nevertheless, three sheets of specimen bold letters (fig.98) were completed by Johnston in December 1929 and sent with an accompanying set of somewhat complex calculations (fig.97) to H. T. Carr, assistant publicity manager.

Making it on Broadway

While Johnston was focusing on his bold lettering, Gill – in the midst of his work for Monotype – transported his family from its remote rural outpost to the Home Counties commuter belt. On 11 October 1928, they moved from Capel-y-ffin in Wales to Piggotts Farm, near High Wycombe in Buckinghamshire. It was not a return to urban living as such, more a copy of the set-up at Capel, with the advantage of a much easier commute to London and the space to set up a separate stone workshop and a printing press with the printer and scholar René Hague (1905–81). One of the first commissions to be executed at Pigotts were three of eight sculptures on the theme of the wind for Holden's new Underground headquarters at 55 Broadway, a project that led to a later commission for two statues to feature on the art deco Broadcasting House, completed in 1932.

For the signage inside 55 Broadway, Pick commissioned Percy Delf Smith, another former student of Johnston's lettering classes, to develop a slightly more ornamental variant of the Standard Alphabet with what were termed petits-serifs (fig.100). Although little survives of it inside the building (which opened between 1928 and 1929), use of the lettering was permitted for a few limited occasions on the new Piccadilly line (fig.102). Delf Smith himself used it for signage inside the new Broadcasting House (fig.99) and developed a lower case that was employed for the signage at the University of London's Torrington House (fig.123).

99

Inside the new Broadcasting House on London's Portland Place, much of the original lettering consisted of either Gill Sans (letters set in relief for 'STUDIO' directions) or hand-painted signs, as here, based on Delf Smith's petits-serifs.

100 (right)

A print-out of Delf Smith lettering from 1929. Pick wanted to reserve the typeface solely for the Underground headquarters at 55 Broadway, but it crept into other areas of London Transport, especially the Piccadilly line extension works.

101 (far right)

Print-out of the sans serif version of his typeface that Delf Smith was called upon to produce and which was used by Southampton Civic Centre when it opened in 1932.

Continental drift

Delf Smith was soon to shine again, in a different architectural context this time. In preparation for major upcoming extensions of the Piccadilly line, Pick visited Berlin in January 1930, and took Holden and W. P. N. Edwards, secretary to Albert Stanley (now Lord Ashfield), with him during the summer of 1930 for a longer fact-finding tour of Continental transportation operations. They visited Denmark, Sweden and the Netherlands, where they were particularly impressed by the way architects were constructing all functions of a building in one united whole, from lighting to signage. They also went to Germany, being especially taken with the Hamburg Hochbahn and the Berlin U-Bahn station architecture of Alfred Grenander (1863–1931).[12] Edwards circulated a report highlighting their desire, as historian David Lawrence puts it, to 'move away from the engineer-led method of producing a railway system, being one of the first Underground reports to focus on design rather than pragmatism and mechanical matters'. Lawrence describes the trip as less a blueprint than a manifesto, a framework of ideals.[13] The first station to undergo the new approach was Sudbury Town. Built in just seven months, it was ready by July 1931. Pick had already decided that the importance of this project was such that it merited use of the specially created Delf Smith petits-serifs for signage (fig.102).

Spaces on the architrave and above the canopy were designed from the outset to hold the Johnston lettering for station names and other details at Northfields, Sudbury Hill and Chiswick Park, which all followed in rapid succession during 1932, all radical in their own way, though the enormous glass and brick drum at

102

Sudbury Town employed the Delf Smith lettering (still preserved today) on the bull's-eye and platform signage.

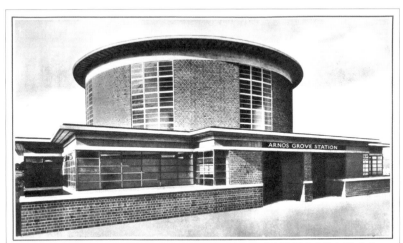

103

Signage for the other stations to open on the Piccadilly line extension were in Johnston lettering and were promoted using the Standard Alphabet, as in this poster from the time with its photograph of Arnos Grove.

104 (opposite)

Delf Smith's petits-serifs are in evidence again on this 1932 poster evoking the breadth of the British Empire.

105 (above left)

Even the Combine was not averse to typeface combinations: an Easter poster for 1932 mixes Gill Sans and Johnston together – perhaps not so surprising given the range of different modes of transport it was publicising?

106 (above right)

On the eve of the Metropolitan being absorbed into the Underground group (p.111) came a striking reminder of its independence: the Met decided to promote the new Piccadilly line stations as being accessible from their red-diamond emblazoned stations . . . with the whole poster set in Gill Sans.

A type-specimen cover of 1929 from the publisher of this book, an early adopter of Gill Sans Titling capitals.

108 (above right)

Edition no.VII of *The Fleuron*, November 1930, offered an exquisitely set sample of Gill Sans Titling in Latin, possibly prepared by Gill himself.

109 (opposite top)

Both Gill and Monotype worked on alternate glyphs for many characters.

Chiswick Park became a model for other stations. Publicity for these Piccadilly extensions was gushing if a bit muddled typographically; one used only Gill Sans, others mixed types which presumably did not please Pick (figs 104–6). Beside this, however, these early station buildings set a trend whose influence extended right up to the Second War World and beyond.

Praise for Gill

No sooner had printers acquired the new Gill Sans typeface than they were keen to try it out in other ways. One of the first off the mark, in 1929, was the publisher of this book, Lund Humphries (fig.107). Gill Sans represented such a revolution in British typesetting at the time that it received much critical acclaim from serious designers. The final edition of the respected *Fleuron*, November 1930, was devoted to a discussion of Gill's type designs (in a long article by Warde, again under the pseudonym Beaujon) and included a page of Latin set in Gill Sans (fig.108). The previous edition (no.VI, from 1928) had given several taster samples of the typeface.

A foolproof alphabet

Neither the Gill nor the Johnston lettering has been immune to criticism, however. Indeed, it could be said that neither man was the most obvious candidate for creating a typeface that would shape the look of modern Britain. Johnston had successfully rekindled an interest in the dying art of handwritten letters using quill and ink, and Gill was obsessed with the almost romantic concept of craftsmanship over industrialisation. Gill's vision was clear, however, and despite the recent loss of his mother, in 1929, and subsequent health issues of his own, the first signs of which appeared in 1930, he decided to put his thoughts down on paper. Dictating the text to René Hague, Gill started work in November 1930 on what would become his *Essay on Typography* (published in 1931). Despite its rather hectoring tone, including tirades against the modern world and the evils of justified text, it offers some wonderful insights, such as the classic quote 'Letters are signs for sounds'.[14] Gill saw his own work as a development of what had preceded it, as revealed by his comments on Johnston's sans serif: '[the] letters are not entirely satisfactory, especially when it is remembered that, for such a purpose, an alphabet should be as near as possible fool-proof'.[15] In his view, his own sans serif was 'perhaps an improvement' on that of his former teacher.[16]

While Johnston is not known to have responded to this, modern critics like Ben Archer have taken issue with Gill here. Regarding his lower case 'a', for example, Archer says that 'the more rational forms are the ones that didn't make the final cut'[17] – although this was perhaps more to do with Monotype than its designer. Archer is not keen on Gill's deletion of the foot on Johnston's 'l' (included by Johnston to stop potential confusion between the numeral '1' and lower-case 'l'). Indeed, the resulting ambiguity is one criticism levelled at Gill Sans (fig.110). Johnston's looped 'l' and sheared-off top of the numeral '1' were perhaps more logical, therefore, though an alternative still needed to be worked on by both Johnston and Gill – something that has come in later years. (The Ordnance Survey included a serif on the number '1' in its redrawn version of Gill Sans in the 1970s, and a similar revision was made to Johnston – p.171.) Less controversially, Gill also deleted the terminal endings of the 'b', 'd', 'p' and 'q', and flattened the bowls of them all (apart from the 'b'). Monotype added them back to begin with, but progressively reverted to Gill's original designs

110 (above)

'One is unwell' or 'The first person singular is three?' Johnston and Gill Sans 'l's compared.

Imitation is the greatest form of flattery.
Designed in 1930, and sitting closer to
Johnston than Gill Sans or Curwen Sans,
was a Stephenson Blake typeface called
Granby. A light weight of the typeface,
shown here, was recently acquired by the
collector Anne Maningas.

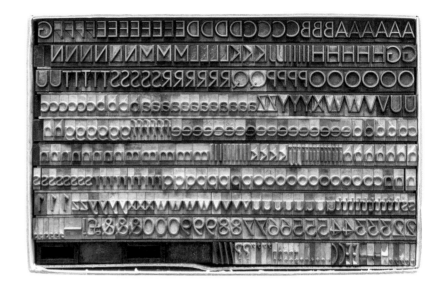

112 (below)

Granby used on the cover of a 1930s
theatre programme from Rhyl in north
Wales.

(except on the light weight). Archer (among others) finds fault with both Gill's
and Johnston's lower-case 'g', though both made alternatives (fig.109).

Any criticism of Gill or Johnston has to be seen in the context of their
overwhelming success, however. Both have been highly influential and a fair
number of similar typefaces have emerged over the years. One that saw the
most use by London Transport as an alternative for Johnston, particularly due to
its similarity to the latter and mainly because of its small point sizes, was Granby
(figs 111–2), designed in 1930 by Sheffield's Stephenson Blake foundry, which had
access to the original Johnston wooden type because they manufactured it. As
Ben Archer concludes: 'The old metal version of Granby has a faithfulness to
Johnston's proportions and characteristics that Eric Gill missed in such a way
as to suggest he did it deliberately. Nearly a century later, Edward Johnston's
pioneering work is still a big noise in contemporary sans serif typeface design.
So much for "fool-proof".'[18]

Gill Sans goes mainstream

As the popularity of Gill Sans began to soar in the early 1930s, so Monotype
looked to further increase the range of weights and styles. By 1932, for example,

a survey of display advertisements in the national press revealed that sans serifs had become by far the most popular kind of typeface. One publication from the time, *Advertising Display*, observed how in 1928 only one advert in a sample of 372 was set in a new sans serif; by 1930 the number had risen to 69 out of 321.[19] No similar surveys are known to have been conducted for other forms of printed material, but a glance at ephemera from the period reveals countless examples of Gill Sans in use. By the early 1930s, there were already 36 branches of the Gill Sans family in Monotype's catalogues alone.

After a series of accents and other special characteristics were added to the typeface, enabling it to be used for setting French, it became known as 'le Gill' in France. In the US, the original Gill Sans Titling became Gill Title. Gill even attempted to develop an Arabic version, but not knowing the language was a major impediment and it meant the type was never cut.

113 (below left)

Gill's fine-tuning of a bold lower-case 's' in April 1931 while the wooden type was in production.

114 (below right)

A page printed recently from a complete set of the wooden Gill Sans type by collector Philip Marriage.

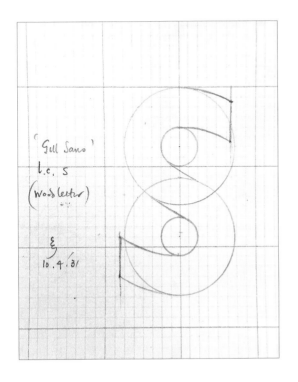

115 (top left)
___
By inking over a trial print-out of the titling caps, Gill experimented with a bolder version in February 1930. Monotype never developed this, but its similarity to a letter shape used later in 1948 (p.138) cannot be ignored.

116 (top right)
___
What would become Gill Sans Extra Bold was made on board in January 1931.

117 (centre)
___
Gill's work on 'shadow line', another variant of the typeface, from 1930. His drawings for Monotype's expansion and improvement of the Gill Sans family continued for several years.

118
___
Gill and LNER executives pose by the *Flying Scotsman* in 1932.

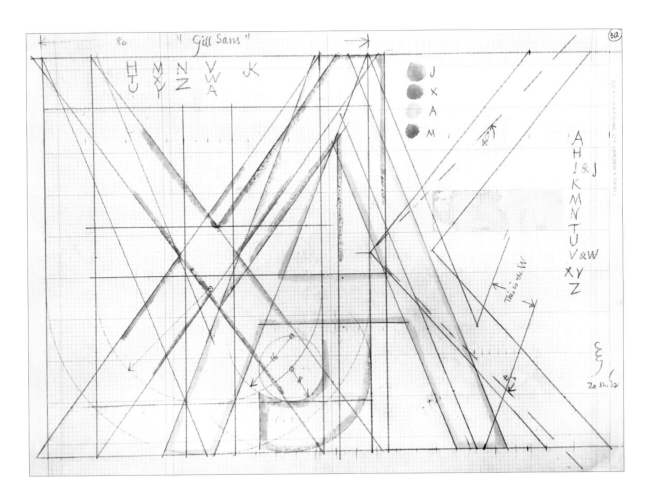

Gill fulfils a boyhood dream

Gill had been fascinated by railways since his childhood, and his early work with Johnston and the subsequent rolling out of lettering he was involved in for the Underground is known to have pleased him. More still, the adoption by the LNER of his own alphabet for their standardisation process (p.92). In 1932 this led to a personal high point for Gill. In recognition of the spread of his lettering across the network, he was asked to personally hand-paint the headboard for the LNER's most famous engine, the *Flying Scotsman* (fig.118). A big enough thrill for any train enthusiast – but to Gill's absolute delight, he was to be given a ride on the engine driver's footplate. Despite his poor health at this time, he wrote with great joy in the LNER's company magazine about the journey from King's Cross to Grantham.[20] Johnston, as far as is known, was never accorded such treats by the Underground. Although neither he nor Gill lived to see it, however, their work was set to go global in the coming decades.

119

Five days before Christmas 1931, for reasons unknown (a seasonal gift?), Gill produced a beautiful mélange of letters labelled 'AHIJKMNTUV&WXYZ'.

Gen: Bk: on Bluiness

2 { shapes — U D &c
   { gen. or Labels

L T

Title p

by E Johnston

Report on the five 'Bull's-eye' Designs for
(Underground Green Line general Tramways Trolley Bus)
Surcharged with the words: London Transport

Part I The Surcharging   Part II The Labels (including the L T Bulls-eye)
[letter spacing or plotting]   [Details worked out]

Part I contd.   P. 2.
The Surcharging of LondT on the B Designs

1. The spacing of the Letters (in London Transport)
                                        26) × 7
On the whole this is very fair but some small adjustments
could be made which would improve them.

The Letters dealt with here are taken from the (approx.) 'Sixinch Bullseye'

LONDON

TRANSPORT
x x   x   x   x   x   x

The stem width
is a bare 7/100 of an inch
So that the measurement
of two in = 15% of stemwidth
not negligible

6

Raising the standard 1933–45

In 1933 the London Passenger Transport Board (LPTB) was created as a public body to oversee every mode of transit in the capital. Its scope was huge: as well as taking over the functions of the former private operators, including all the Underground lines of the UERL, the Metropolitan Railway and the Great Northern & City line, it was now responsible for all the buses and Green Line coaches, 400 miles of tram routes and the new trolleybuses within a radius of about 30 miles of Charing Cross. The operating name was to be London Transport (LT) and this was duly added to all the existing bull's-eyes and designs officially registered in 1934 (fig.121). With the exception of the Green Line services (for obvious reasons), every vehicle from trams to Underground cars was painted red. At the same time, new stations were opening on the Southgate extension of the Piccadilly line, such as Cockfosters in 1933, there was a bold new map, and the New Works Programme was projecting to convert many suburban steam routes to Underground electric services. All the lettering for the related signage and publicity was in either Johnston's alphabet (fig.124) or one of its surrogates, Granby (fig.111), Gill Sans (fig.126) or Curwen Sans (fig.93) and even Delf Smith (fig.122). Spreading exponentially across London and the Home Counties, the new sans serifs were having a field day.

120 (opposite)

First page of a report for Pick by Johnston. Prepared in 1933 it was made to assist the newly created London Transport on placement of the bull's-eye elements.

121 (top left)

Exterior of an Underground station photographed in 1940. With Gill Sans Bold visible on the LNER 'winking eye' logo and Johnston's letters resplendent on the bull's-eye beneath, the period saw both typefaces gaining popularity.

122 (top right)

A car park sign at Enfield West (later Oakfield) from 1933–5 in Delf Smith's petits-serifs. Although this typeface was initially intended for use only at the London Transport headquarters, it had been used in 1932 at Sudbury Town (p.101) and later emerged in signage across other stations opened between 1933 and 1935.

123 (second row)

Delf Smith's petits-serifs were also used on signage around Senate House (No.2, Torrington Square, 1937) and included some lower case that appears to be a cross between Johnston and Gill Sans.

124 (third row)

It was during the early 1930s that the Johnston letters were extended to the Metropolitan line, as shown in this drawing of how the logo should be displayed from the Mechanical Engineers Office, with enlarged first and last letters.

125 (bottom)

Taking more liberties, this early 1930s fuse wire holder was made by the North Metropolitan Electrical Supply Company.

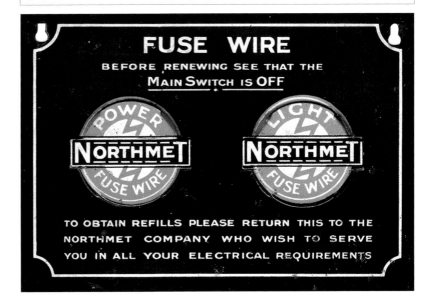

Nearest stations
PUTNEY BRIDGE
HAMMERSMITH
RAVENSCOURT PK.
TURNHAM GREEN
CHISWICK PARK
Bus routes
9, 11, 14, 22, 27, 30
32, 33, 55, 73, 74, 85
93, 96, 127, 173
255, 273, 291, 373
Tram routes
26, 28, 30, 57, 63
67, 89

BOAT RACE MARCH 17 - 2.30

126

This 1934 poster by Anna Katrina Zinkeisen
for the Oxford and Cambridge Boat Race
combines Johnston for display type and a
hand-rendered approximation of Gill Sans
for the text in the centre.

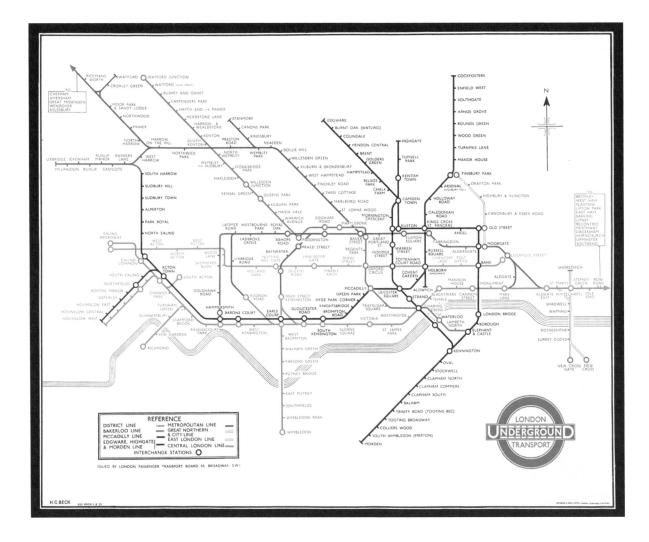

127

The first quad royal poster of the new Underground map, 1933. The bull's-eye with 'London Transport' appears to have been pasted on afterwards, presumably covering the original version. Unlike the pocket map, here all the lettering was set in Johnston.

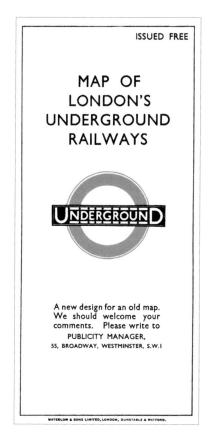

New maps for old

Given the newness of the LPTB, the bold steps it was taking in architecture, such as at Southgate and Boston Manor, and with Pick's continuing tradition of fresh poster design, the moment was right for a brand new map of the Underground. The initiative did not come from above, however. Instead it was seized by a lowly engineer, Henry Beck (1902–74), who in 1931 presented the Board with his new take on mapping the system (fig.127). Historian Ken Garland, who interviewed Beck, rightly cites him as the originator of the entire diagrammatic concept,[1] though the idea was not without precedent. Beck would certainly have been aware of the simplified strip maps present at the time in Tube cars and railway carriages, and possibly also George Dow's diagrammatic designs for the LNER. Beck's initial draft was rejected, but he was persistent and the Board first published his design in 1933 as a pocket map. Set in Gill Sans, a note on the cover for the new map asked for comments (figs 128–9) and Beck then drew larger versions for the posters in stations, this time set in Johnston lettering. Clear and authoritative, the new design not only altered how Londoners saw their city, but went on to become a blueprint for transport maps around the world.

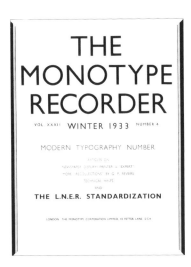

LNER's mass conversion

Monotype's in-house journal, the *Monotype Recorder*, ran a major feature on the LNER standardisation in 1933 (fig.130) and its benefits, observing how the railway company's myriad timetables, pamphlets and notices formed a 'cumulative impression'.[2] Though 'a great many . . . had to be dragooned into co-operation',[3] the conversion to Monotype's Gill Sans of all the printers that supplied the LNER led to a more unified look typographically for LNER printed material than for any other mainline railway, and played a major role in popularising and expanding the range of the typeface family. The *Recorder* indicates that the LNER's first newspaper ads (p.94) had been 'set in "Monotype" Gill Sans for testing purposes', as 'the lower case . . . and the great range of bold, extra bold, bold condensed and extra light in roman and italic depended to some extent on the success of the magnificent titling capitals'.[4] The LNER, which also commissioned Gill to redesign its own logo (fig.132), effectively forced the early success and expansion of Gill Sans.

The three other British mainline railway companies – all equally prolific producers of printed ephemera – not only watched the LNER's adoption of Gill Sans with a degree of awe, but several of them took to using it themselves (fig.134).

130 (above)

Reporting on the LNER standardisation in 1933, the *Monotype Recorder* barely needed to overplay the growing popularity of Gill Sans. The July 1933 cover of *Design for Today*, which used an outline version of Gill Sans as its masthead for some years.

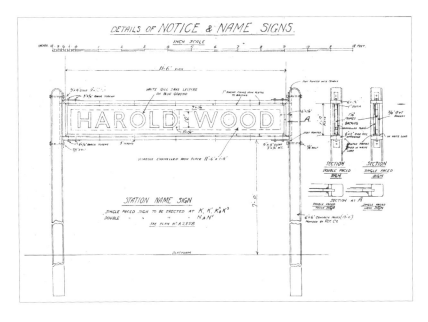

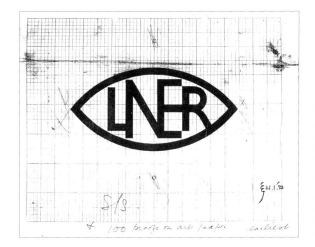

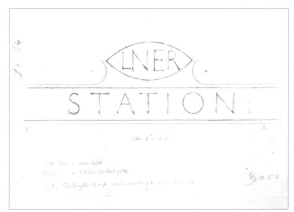

131 (opposite)

Architect's drawing detail for the rebuild and re-signing of the London and North Eastern Railway's (LNER) Harold Wood station shows meticulous attention to the use of in-house lettering, echoed later in London Transport's Carr-Edwards report (p.127).

132 (above)

Gill's designs for the LNER logo, showing (top left) his first attempt of 1933 with letters touching each other, superseded by the final version (top right and second row) in 1936. Known as the 'winking eye', it was used extensively between 1934 and 1948, becoming one of the best-known railway logos.

133 (above left)
_____

A London Midland and Scottish Railway poster advertising holiday tickets to the Lake District, c.1933. The mid 1930s saw other railway companies begin to use a lot of Gill Sans.

134 (above right)
_____

The only known appearance in colour of London Passenger Transport Board's (LPTB) winged circle device, which was considered as a replacement for the bull's-eye logo. Stylised Curwen Sans has been used for headlines with Johnston permitted for the logo, station names and ticket prices.

135

The Great Western Railway (GWR) used Gill Sans for some display work, as exemplified by this
1939 'Speed to the West' promotion illustrated by Charles Mayo.

A 1938 safety poster by Imperial Airways. The burgeoning commercial airline industry was another early adopter of Gill Sans. Imperial Airways (in existence between 1924 and 1939) was perhaps the most frequent user, with virtually all its printed material, from baggage labels to advertising, being set in Gill Sans from the early 1930s.

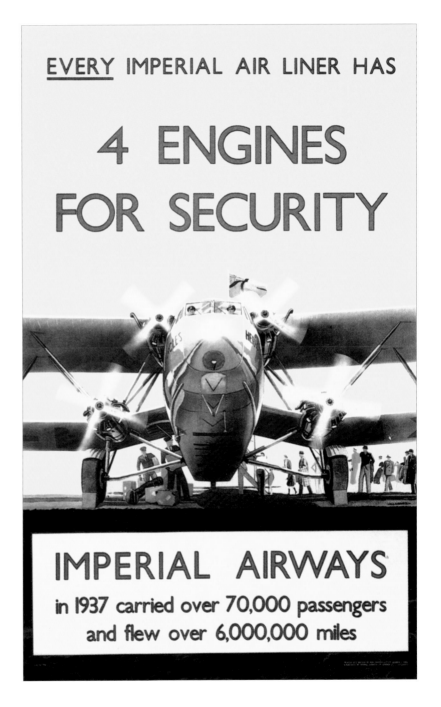

EVERY IMPERIAL AIR LINER HAS

4 ENGINES FOR SECURITY

IMPERIAL AIRWAYS

in 1937 carried over 70,000 passengers and flew over 6,000,000 miles

137 (left)

Max Gill's roundel logo for the General Post Office (GPO), using his brother's Gill Sans typeface. His first design, incorporating two concentric circles (see top left and right), was featured on only a handful of early publications in 1934. The finalised logo appeared on everything produced by the GPO.

138 (below)

The Post Office was a major user of Gill Sans. The Condensed weight was hand-painted onto the sides of thousands of vehicles from the mid 1930s onwards.

They also produced a number of joint posters, sometimes with just a couple working together, the London, Midland and Scottish Railway (LMS) more often than not with the LNER, and the Great Western Railway (GWR) with the Southern Railway (SR) – good geographical allies. While these were not always in Gill Sans, joint posters made in the name of all four companies invariably featured the typeface. Taking their cue from the LNER in adopting Gill Sans for posters, timetables and handbills, the other three companies also attempted to create their own logos in a sans serif face, the one for the GWR being the most distinctive.

The GPO and Penguin follow suit

With sans serifs being increasingly adopted by large corporate bodies (including the burgeoning airline industry, fig.136), Gill Sans was an obvious choice for the General Post Office (GPO), which had grown to encompass banking and telephone services. Following the LNER's lead, it developed a Gill Sans-based

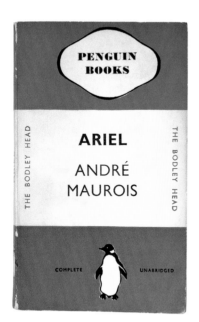

139

The very first title published in 1935 under the new Penguin Books imprint, featuring the iconic cover in Gill Sans lettering for all but the publisher's name in the top cartouche.

logo, commissioned in 1934 from Gill's brother Max (1884–1947), a distinguished designer in his own right. It was not out of any family loyalty that Max chose to use Gill's typeface but because it conveyed the requisite gravitas for such an august institution. In the original design, he allowed space for the full stops after the 'G' and 'P', but as the one after the 'O' would have been obliterated or created a nasty clash with the double circular band around the logo, all full stops were left off the first printed versions. The logo was certainly effective, but GPO designers soon asked Max for a simpler version with just one concentric band. The letters – especially the letter 'G' – were also slightly revised while remaining essentially Gill Sans (fig.137). Appearing on millions of items, from telephone directories, stamp books and other printed ephemera to productions by the GPO's film unit, the logo lasted until the early 1950s when it was completely redesigned.

Book publishing then took up the trend, albeit one that had already kicked off overseas. Launched in Germany in 1932, the Albatross imprint was devoted to publishing English books in territories outside the USA or the British Empire. They appeared in eye-catching covers with lettering set in the clear Futura sans serif typeface. Making their first appearance in 1935, Penguin Books aimed to bring literature to the British mass market with cheaper paperbacks. Taking its inspiration from Albatross, Penguin's production manager, Edward Preston Young, divided the cover horizontally into three sections, with a thick band of colour at the top and bottom for displaying the publisher's name and logo (designed by Young) and white middle layer for the author's name and book title. The first publication in the new imprint (fig.139) featured Gill Sans for all cover text except the 'PENGUIN BOOKS' logo – and even this was replaced by Gill Sans when the design was refined in 1948 by Jan Tschichold. By contrast, Pelican Books, launched in 1937, used Gill Sans for the whole cover from the outset. The initial simple design for Penguin Books, and revision using Gill Sans, set the standard until it was replaced in 1961, though the design of those early books has proved so iconic that it is periodically revived.

Emboldening Gill

Behind the scenes at Monotype, Gill Sans was being constantly adjusted in response to demand, with new weights being added as required. As Gill specialist Sallie Morris comments:

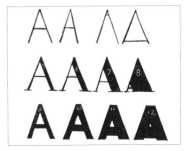

140 (left)

Reverse of Monotype's specimen release of Gill Kayo in 1935.

141 (above)

A drawing from Gill's *Essay on Typography* showing the emboldening of an 'A' to the point at which it would look ludicrous.

Each time Monotype developed new sizes of an existing type design, it brought fresh scrutiny on the design. Hence the tweaking that went on for decades. This is true of all their type designs, not just Gill's. If additional sizes were being produced it generally meant Monotype had received a request for them or anticipated a demand for them.[5]

Gill Sans Extra Bold had proved a winner with printers, so Monotype asked Gill to work on an even heavier letterform for such applications as poster display. In his *Essay on Typography* Gill discusses the 'boldening' of an 'A' (fig.141), as Johnston had done in his notes to students, indicating that he was not entirely

A type specimen showing the huge range of Gill Sans that was available by the mid 1930s, including Cameo, Ruled, Bold Condensed Titling and Shadow Line. At times Monotype was rushing out new weights so fast that they barely merited a mention in the *Recorder*. Note that what was marketed as Gill Kayo was named 'Gill Ultra Bold' here.

GILL SANS. A 'Monotype' *face* of a

GILL BOLD and ***Gill Bold Italic***

GILL BOLD CONDENSED an attractive

Gill Sans CONDENSED Series No. 485 is a real saving

GILL SANS Light *and italic* ABab

GILL SANS Extra Bold ABab

GILL BOLD CONDENSED TITLING NO. I

Gill Sans Shadow Line for unique dis

GILL SHADOW 406

GILL ULTRA Bold abcfgi

This is 'Monotype' Gill Sans Bold EXTRA CONDENSED abcdefghi

GILL CAMEO ?!?" |—|

GILL SANS 231 TITLING CAPITA

happy about the process of thickening letters, calling, for example, 11 'Sans over-bold' and 12 'hardly recognizable'.[6] In February 1933 he made some ink drawings for Monotype which he labelled 'sans double-elefans', causing some to speculate that it was done as a bit of a joke, or certainly that he did not envisage it as part of the graceful Gill Sans family. Monotype must have agreed with him as they released it in 1935 as 'Gill Kayo' – i.e. 'KO', short for 'knockout' – rather than 'Gill Sans Kayo' (fig.140). Because it was so unconventional, the new typeface has not always met with universal approval, however, and critics have been quite disparaging: 'Typographical historians of 2000 AD (which isn't, after all, so very far away) will find this an odd outburst in Mr Gill's career, and will spend much time in attempting to track down this sad psychological state of his during 1936'.[7]

That Edward Johnston was commissioned in 1917 to design the sanserif type in which this announcement is set (the forerunner of the twentieth-century revivals of this letter-form) —that Feliks Topolski was commissioned last year to draw a series of character studies—these are but two examples of London Transport's consistent policy of a keen and practical interest in sound presentation. Advertise, therefore, in good company through London Transport's vehicles, stations and publications to 9,500,000 people.

LONDON TRANSPORT 55 BROADWAY S W 1   VICTORIA 6800

A CAR PANEL ON THE UNDERGROUND

COST 1⁰ to 1½⁰ PER DAY

SIZE 10½in. x 23½in. (UPRIGHT)

ENQUIRIES TO COMMERCIAL ADVERTISING OFFICER

55 BROADWAY S.W.1   VIC 6000

143 (far left)

This 1935 advert for placing billboards inside carriages is set in Curwen Sans. As the lower case was quite exotic, the typeface was not ideal as a substitute, but after Gill Sans and Granby the capitals were the third most frequently used for London Transport work in place of Johnston. Indeed at times, especially during the mid 1930s, Curwen Sans was seen more often than Gill Sans.

144 (above right)

By the time of this 1937 advert praising the typeface, a few more sizes of Johnston were available to printers.

Even if an extra bold would not have been Gill's choice for a typeface, he rarely turned down a commission. As Morris comments: 'Gill was pragmatic about doing various jobs as long as it brought in money.'[8] Gill Kayo was followed by the more sober Gill Bold Condensed for Post Office Telephones, a client of Monotype, and in 1937 the Extra Condensed. Gill may have been inclined to call it a day at this point, but Monotype had other ideas (fig.142).

Substitutes for Johnston

One of the major problems for London Transport and their printers was the limitations of the original Standard Alphabet, not just in the bold – as touched on in the previous chapter – but in the range of different sizes available, especially at the smaller end. As a result, substitutions – mostly for body copy – were frequently made, often driven by necessity, because there was nothing in the printer's drawers for producing lettering that was sufficiently small. One of the faces that was most frequently substituted for it, therefore, was Gill Sans, partly due to the myriad point sizes available and partly, as former UK director type at Monotype Dan Rhatigan says, 'thanks to the success of Monotype in spreading the typeface so far and wide'.[9] The others were Granby and Curwen Sans (fig.143). Despite the time and money they had previously spent developing and protecting the Johnston alphabet, LPTB, from its inception in 1933, experimented quite liberally with Curwen Sans especially on printed ephemera, though never on signage, it seems. At the same time, the Johnston range was being both expanded (fig.144) and applications for its use more strictly categorised. Like Gill Sans at LNER, the Johnston alphabet was about to undergo its own standardisation.

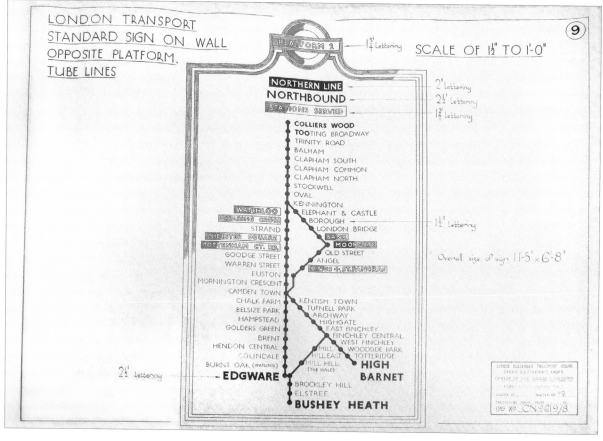

JOHNSTON & GILL

Johnston standardised

Despite the greatest efforts of Pick and Carr and many others at the LPTB, the quality of signage across London Transport was not as uniform as they had hoped. Moreover, the network was about to be joined, in 1935, by a whole swathe of extra lines and stations under the proposed New Works Programme (NWP) (fig.146). This would require a vast array of signage, not just for the new stations but also for existing lines, as, for instance, where new interchanges demanded revised direction panels. There was also the thorny issue of where precisely the words 'LONDON' and 'TRANSPORT' should best be displayed on a sign and Johnston had suggestions (fig.120). Although the bus lettering was revised in 1937 by Henry Carter, the rules for other questions came in a document named after its authors. The Carr–Edwards report of 1938, widely regarded as one of the first corporate-identity manuals, set out how the Johnston Standard Alphabet should be used, including where station names were to be positioned. It was accompanied by a large book of hand-coloured drawings known as *Standard Signs* (fig.147) which prescribed in great detail the size, shape and style of lettering to be adopted.

145 (opposite top left)

A 1940 poster eulogising the Johnston alphabet was the first of its kind to be widely distributed.

146 (opposite top right)

The platform at St John's Wood photographed in December 1939. Only small sections of the extended Tube network proposed by the New Works Programme were opened before the war. These included the Bakerloo extension to Finchley Road, with two new intermediate stations at St John's Wood and Swiss Cottage, both with signage complying to the standards laid out in the 1938 Carr–Edwards report.

147 (opposite bottom)

Specification for lettering for a line diagram in a page from the 1938 Carr–Edwards report, commissioned by the LPTB in an attempt to create visual uniformity across bus, tram and Tube networks.

148 (above)

'Twentieth Century Block Lettering Based Upon Roman Proportion': sample from Leonard Charles Evetts's book *Roman Lettering* of 1938, showing how, aside from Granby and Curwen Sans, several other typefaces were being developed at this time that bore a resemblance to Johnston and Gill Sans.

149

The London and North Eastern Railway's (LNER) *Mallard* and *Bittern* steam locomotives with nameplates in Gill Sans. Heavily promoted by the railway companies as part of their marketing, iconic locomotives such as these embodied the streamlined era of the 1930s. LNER's Silver Jubilee class (1935) was outpaced by the London Midland and Scottish Railway's (LMS) *Coronation Scot* (1937), which in turn was beaten by the *Mallard* (1938).

150 (opposite, top row two left)

Mock-ups of LNER posters in Gill Sans produced in September 1939. Surprisingly, much of it was made in the correct typeface for each institution.

151 (opposite, top row two right)

Conflicting advice on London Underground posters. The first in Johnston, November 1939, is overruled by another, in 1940, which ended up in Gill Sans.

Full steam ahead

In matters of corporate identity, the mainline railways were not resting on their laurels either. At the LNER, Cecil Dandridge and William M. Teasdale, much like Pick 20 years earlier, were not driven simply by the desire to make things look good for the sake of it. There was a lot more at stake. The Wall Street Crash of 1929 and the ensuing Great Depression of the 1930s affected Europe as much as the US, and the railways were also contending now with increasing competition from the motor car as a mode of transport. As a result, rail company executives and their publicity departments were putting a concerted effort into promoting the train lines. The Silver Jubilee of King George V in 1935, partly intended as a morale-boosting jamboree and partly to divert attention from the ominous storm clouds over Europe, also provided excellent publicity for the railways. The LNER named a service after the event, using their Class A4 locomotives, promoting it with stylish printed material and newspaper advertising. The introduction by the LMS of the rival Coronation Class locomotives in 1937 was intended to give them the edge in the lucrative market of passengers on the mainline between London, the Midlands, the North West and Scotland. The streamlined style of these sleek modern steam locomotives seemed to capture the spirit of the age. Both routes were heavily marketed using impressive graphics, for which a modern sans serif was de rigueur. The LNER's *Mallard*, with lettering in Gill Sans, of course (fig.149), performed a record-breaking steam speed run in July 1938, reaching 126mph (200kph), a feat that was itself publicised to encourage passenger traffic (and a record still unbroken).

Putting on a brave face

The onset of war brought everything to a grinding halt, however, and the 'Big Four' were brought under government control. It was from this point that the words 'British Railways' were seen on posters beneath the initials of the rail companies, a collective name that was to rise to the fore after the hostilities ceased. Lettering on the posters was still mostly in Gill Sans.

Both the Johnston and Gill typefaces were co-opted as part of the war effort, especially in public information notices giving advice on what to do during a blackout or in an air raid (figs 150–1). Sans serifs regularly featured in propaganda too, as exemplified by a series of three posters produced on the eve of the Second World War by the Ministry of Information. Rediscovered in

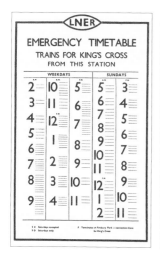

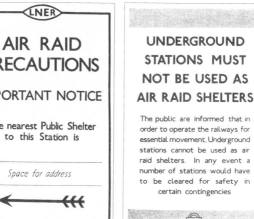

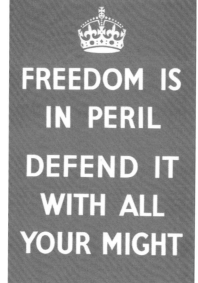

152 (above, second row)

Rediscovered in 2000 in a Northumbrian shop, Barter Books, the original 'KEEP CALM AND CARRY ON' poster (left) from 1939 was never set in Gill Sans, although is widely assumed to have been. Another of three wartime posters issued by the Home Office and reflecting their advice for a 'special and handsome typeface' that would be hard for enemies to replicate (centre). Other wartime posters were set in Gill Sans (right).

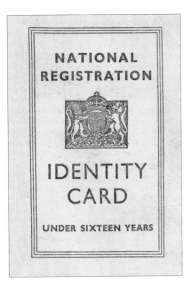

MINISTRY OF FOOD

**RATION BOOK
SUPPLEMENT**

PAGE 1

OFFICIAL PAID

This is a Spare Book

**YOU WILL BE TOLD
HOW AND WHEN TO USE IT**

HOLDER'S NAME AND REGISTERED ADDRESS

Surname..
Other Names...
Address..

If found, please return to | NATIONAL REGISTRATION NO.

FOOD OFFICE. | Class and Serial No. of Ration
Book already held

Date of Issue............ | R.B.9

153

Ration book and identity card. From the Second World War onwards, hundreds of official documents were printed in Gill Sans, from call-up papers and Post Office telegrams to posters and pamphlets.

2000, the first of these was reissued in Gill Sans (fig.152), although the original would have been written in a more generic, hand-drawn sans serif. Almost two and half million copies of the morale-boosting advice to 'KEEP CALM AND CARRY ON' were printed in the summer of 1939, but not approved for immediate issue. Instead two others, 'FREEDOM IS IN PERIL' and 'YOUR COURAGE', were prioritized for distribution, while the majority of the 'KEEP CALM' ones were never issued and later pulped.

During the conflict itself, but even more in the years of austerity that followed, so many official and government documents were produced using Gill Sans (fig.153), which fulfilled this function with such ease and authority, that it strongly tilted the British psyche into thinking that it must be an official form of lettering.

Beginning of the end

While their lettering was in robust health, the same could not be said of the men themselves during this period. Like Gill, Johnston had been ailing, the most debilitating complaint for a graphic artist being his failing sight, and he was frequently bedridden, as a result of which he took on very little work. In 1936, his wife Greta died. After the funeral, Gill penned heartfelt condolences to Johnston, in what turned out to be his final communication with his old friend. Unashamedly quoting from his own diary, Gill proclaimed his abiding love for his former teacher, a devotion stretching back to their very first encounter at the lettering classes in 1903. He had been very fond of Greta too. Touchingly admitting that 'your marriage meant more to me than to anyone else in the whole world except you and your wife'. As Priscilla Johnston put it, the letter was 'a fitting conclusion and farewell to a friendship so long and so fruitful'.[10] Johnston spent some of his remaining energy, even while bedridden, attempting to write a follow-up to *Writing & Illuminating & Lettering* but was unable to complete the work. (It was subsequently pulled together by Heather Child and published in 1971, by Lund Humphries, as *Formal Penmanship*.)

In the run-up to the outbreak of war, when well enough, Gill was now giving much of his time over to political thinking, expressed both in writing and public speaking. Always occupied with various activities simultaneously, even at this stage, he also completed the background design for the first definitive stamp series of George VI for the Post Office in 1937 (not using Gill Sans). Gill's last direct contribution to his font family, Bold Extra Condensed, was made three years before he died, in 1937.

Johnston was not able (or not asked) to contribute to the London Underground *Standard Signs* manual. Awarded a CBE for services to calligraphy in 1939, he was unfortunately too unwell to attend the investiture. Incredibly, given his many contributions to modern life, he was also in financial difficulties. However, when colleagues became aware of this, money poured in, which enabled Johnston to employ a nurse to look after him. Even with his health failing, Johnston took on a few last pieces of work. One he was determined to complete was for the retirement of Pick from chairmanship of the LPTB; his inscription on a brown leather blotter was presented to Pick in 1940. One design historian claims Pick's choice of Johnston changed the face of British printing.[11]

Both Johnston and Gill had been less productive, in terms of typography at least, during the last years of their lives, though each remained dedicated to their other projects. Through worsening health in summer 1940, Gill dictated his autobiography, having already cut his own gravestone some time earlier (though that version was not used). He was diagnosed with lung cancer at High Wycombe Hospital in October. Despite initially refusing an operation, one was eventually carried out. Although he recovered a little from surgery, he suffered a relapse and died on Sunday 17 November 1940.

His former teacher outlived him by another four years. Johnston's very last piece of work, in 1944, was a commission that could not be refused despite his own poor health. It was for Winston Churchill: some poignant lines from Shakespeare to be presented to Harry Hopkins, personal representative of President Roosevelt, at a private meeting. Johnston was now so debilitated he could not rise from his bed and had to direct Irene Wellington, a former student of his, to carry out the work. After much effort, Wellington produced such a well-executed manuscript that it elicited the rarest and highest praise from Johnston: 'That's beautiful' – much to the joy of Wellington herself.[12] Johnston died not long afterwards in the Ditchling village he had made his last home. With both artists having passed away, that might have been the end of the story, but the creations of Johnston and Gill had achieved such heights that they had acquired a life and momentum of their own.

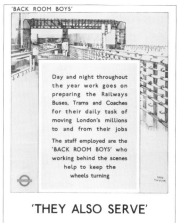

154

One of a series of four posters by Fred Taylor with the caption 'THEY ALSO SERVE' in Johnston lettering, issued by London Transport in 1942 as part of the war effort, in recognition of those who kept things going at home.

For the motorist
whose car is always in use

HILLMAN MINX

A PRODUCT OF THE ROOTES GROUP

7

The face
of authority
1946–79

Britain emerged from six long years of war in a very sorry state. Setting aside the horrific human loss, the country was quite literally in ruins. The bomb damage was bad enough but the Treasury was close to bankruptcy too. Food was initially in shorter supply than during the war and the tiresome daily battle for meagre pickings using ration books and food tokens (much of this material printed using Gill Sans, p.130) added to the misery. Conscription was still in force, reconstruction of homes and services painfully slow and, although the war had been won, morale was desperately low.

Alongside the rebuilding, one of the first jobs was to finish off projects that had been started before the war. In London that meant the completion of the Central line extensions, and these were carried out between 1946 and 1949, with the Johnston lettering much in evidence (fig.157).

Although both Johnston and Gill were now dead, their respective alphabets (and much of their other work) lived on. The use of Gill Sans was about to go stratospheric, appearing on almost every printed surface and building sign, whereas there were mixed fortunes for Johnston's alphabet. When it came to signage for London Transport, Johnston still reigned supreme in the post-war

155 (opposite)

The British motor industry also embraced Gill Sans, as exemplified by this Hillman advertisement from 1947.

Paddington station, photographed in 1955, with Underground signage in Johnston and British Railways architrave lettering in Gill Sans. New signs featuring both Johnston and BR's Gill Sans were commonplace at shared stations in London.

Mile End station in 1948. Completed after the war, the eastward extension of the Central line, opened between Liverpool Street and Stratford in 1946, was resplendent with Johnston lettering on ceramic tile friezes and, as here, on the fascias of newly rebuilt stations.

period. By 1946 there was not a bus, train, tram, trolleybus, bus stop, Tube station or vehicle garage that did not display the Johnston lettering in some form. And as the rebuilding programme slowly got under way, there was never any question that this style of lettering would remain in use for this function. Signage was protected by the Carr–Edwards *Standard Signs* manual – which was updated in 1948 following an additional report (fig.158). With a view to placing greater emphasis on LT identity as a whole, the only change of substance was a recommendation to expunge the word 'UNDERGROUND' and any mention of 'BUS' on the vehicles and from official signs and replace it with the words 'LONDON TRANSPORT'.[1] Printed material was a different matter, however. Unofficially, and for some years, printers had been substituting Johnston with Gill Sans and Curwen Sans, and a few other typefaces, to provide the smaller point sizes, but this was now becoming officially enshrined into the design briefs from the Underground publicity office.

For Gill Sans the reverse was true: it was becoming ubiquitous. Change was mostly driven by the full nationalisation of all rail, canal, docks and road haulage operations under the British Transport Commission (1 January 1948) and the

more used than the main entrance because the peak hour traffic funnels through them more naturally. Here is a sample stairwell :-

Here the recommended standard needs modification. The name of the station can be clearly marked as it is at Tottenham Court Road Station by an illuminated sign underneath the bullseye and the bullseye itself should therefore read 'London Transport'. The new stairwell would, therefore look like this :-

and it should be noted that there is an excellent position .er o secondary sign telling the public as they enter that the subway leads not only to the District and Circle Lines and the Southern Region station but also to trams and public lavatories.

Bank Station by similar logic would be changed from :-

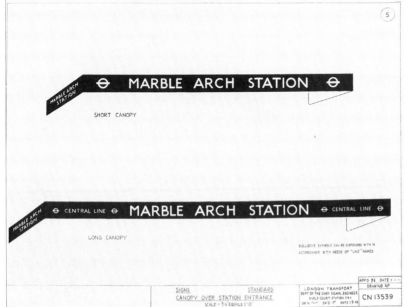

158

Pages from the Carr–Edwards report of 1948, showing how revisions to signage were to be implemented. Post-nationalisation the words 'UNDERGROUND' were replaced with 'LONDON TRANSPORT'. A revised *Standard Signs* manual was produced (completed in 1951 and progressively added to) showing how revisions to lettering should be applied, with white lettering added to station photos to indicate where the changes should be made. Bus stops and vehicles were to be given the full London Transport treatment too.

British Road Services (BRS) vehicles from the late 1940s (top) and 1950s (bottom) with lettering in Johnston, which appeared on vans and garages (including those of its Parcels Services division) until 1969, when BRS was rebranded as the National Freight Company.

unified approach to printed material that this demanded. This was followed by the founding of the National Health Service in July the same year. Other nationalised industries at this time included the Central Electricity Authority, British Transport Docks, British Road Services (BRS), Pickfords and Thomas Cook & Son. BRS was one of the very few companies permitted to use the precious Johnston lettering – on the painted signs on their vans and depots (fig.159); for almost every other major institution at this time, Gill Sans was the typeface of choice.

The Big Four unite

If the LNER standardisation was the trigger for Gill Sans going public in the late 1920s, then the adoption of it for all railways in Britain in 1948 was, in some ways, its twenty-first birthday celebration. As part of the Labour government's nationalisation of all mass transport (which came into effect on 1 January 1948), all the assets of the Big Four (LNER, LMS, SR and GWR) were taken over by the British Transport Commission whose railway executive was to run them under the name of British Railways. (The term had already been in use both before and during the war, when the government had taken control of the railways, and it had appeared on posters in Gill Sans lettering, fig.160.) The new organisation clearly required a unified look and with much of the old Big Four already using Gill Sans, and the knowledge that hundreds of printers were already equipped with the typeface, it was a natural step for the executive to opt for it. Taking a leaf out of London Underground's book, the board prepared its own *Sign Standards* manual, which was ready by April 1948. With Gill Sans forming the bedrock of the report, its guidelines were unequivocally clear and, again replicating the London Underground, a logo was to be used both for station name signs and as the operating symbol for British Railways.

Although the entire document was printed in green (fig.161), it was not intended that the signage at every station in the country would be in that colour. Six geographic regions had been created and they were each allocated their own livery, in which the new enamel signs and printed material would be made: Eastern (Medium Blue), Northern Eastern (Orange Peel), London Midland (Free Speech Red), Scottish (Dodger Blue), Southern (Salem Green) and Western (Peru Tan).

The installation of these signs on thousands of railway premises across the whole of the country (up to 10,000 in total), combined with the use of Gill Sans on millions of pieces of printed ephemera, was one of the defining moments for this typeface and probably did more to weld it into the national consciousness than in anything else up to that point.

Signs of recovery

Nationalisation played a big part in the development of modern signage, much of it featuring Gill Sans in some form. In a broader context, it was three important public events that took place between 1948 and 1953 that were to shape Britain's

160

Travel brochure (all set in Gill Sans Bold) for the North American market issued in the late 1930s. It was one of many occassions where the Big Four were collectively branded as 'British Railways' prior to nationalisation.

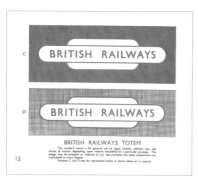

161

Lettering and signage from British Railways' 1948 *Sign Standards* manual. The specified weight, 'Gill Sans Medium Letters', was very specific for its epoch and has been difficult to reproduce today as it doesn't match any known weight. The closest to be found is Gill Sans Poster or Monotype's trial bold (p.108), but even these are not identical. Modern reproductions are easily spotted, therefore. A boon for collectors, the original signs (one for each region shown in correct colours, bottom row) can fetch big prices at auction.

cultural landscape, with a major contribution to the evolution of contemporary British design as a whole. These were the Olympic Games (1948), the Festival of Britain (1951) and the coronation of Queen Elizabeth II (1953) – all centred on the capital but each with some regional activity. Anyone who witnessed the elaborate organisation of the 2012 Olympic Games in London (p.176) would be amazed by the idea of hosting such a complex activity in a city still ravaged by bomb damage and recovering from war. But with a sense of solidarity and a strong community spirit (oddly not dissimilar to that which emerged 60 years later) the Games were a great success. Thousands of volunteers (including the author's Boy Scout father) helped visitors navigate the ruins to Wembley, guided by the clarity of special signage on public transport, all set in Johnston lettering (fig.162). Standing on the shoulders of the 1936 Berlin Games, the event was also broadcast on live television and radio by the BBC, which equipped a temporary structure, the Palace of Arts, and featured sans serif letters for 'BROADCASTING CENTRE' on the architrave. Commemorative stamps were issued for the occasion, although despite going through several drafts none eventually featured Gill Sans.

The Festival of Britain was seen as a great boost to morale: there were ten million paid entries, with eight million visiting the main South Bank site alone. Dedicated to a review of contemporary achievement in British industry, this venue included an exhibition on design and craftsmanship. Graphic presentation of the Festival as a whole was considered important, the lettering style being overseen by a typography panel assembled for the occasion. A typeface was specially commissioned for exhibition display. Designed in a decorative visual style by Phillip Boydell, its condensed italic and open form seeming to embrace elements of Gill Condensed and Inline, it was known as Festival Titling (fig.164). Gill Sans itself was used extensively for signage at all the exhibition sites, and on temporary road signs directing traffic to the event (fig.163).

The Festival really did seem to be ushering in another age as it was closely followed, on 2 June 1953, by the coronation of a new monarch, Elizabeth II. An avalanche of souvenirs, printed matter, maps and guides were produced for what became one of the greatest public occasions of twentieth-century Britain, much of it presented in Gill Sans.

Such was the versatility of the Gill lettering, in fact, that it was fast becoming embedded in everyday life. By the late 1940s and early 1950s, manufacturing and

162

Temporary signage directing visitors to the Olympic Games venue at Wembley in 1948 was erected across London in Johnston bold and regular lettering in English and, in some places, French.

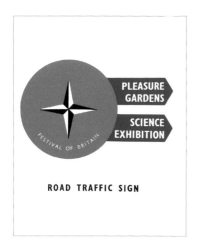

163

The Festival of Britain issued a booklet for organisers of events across the country to assist them in making unified signage in 'Standardized Lettering'. The main typeface was Gill Sans Bold Condensed.

industry were beginning to recover. During this period an increasing array of products were being labelled in Gill Sans, from machine tools to domestic gadgets, administrative documents to advertisements, shopfronts to food packaging. The caseroom of virtually every printer in Britain had trays of Gill Sans; it was seen by the trade, as Morison had hoped it would be, as the standard, neat, clean jobbing face for most display ads and labelling. Dan Rhatigan suggests that it was this period that cemented both Gill and Johnston – the latter seen by millions of passengers on their way through London – as the go-to typefaces for England.[2]

Typecast for television

The three public spectacles of the Olympics, the Festival of Britain and the Coronation helped usher in a period of growing prosperity. Food rationing ended in 1954, the economy (in the US especially) was improving and a new era seemed to be dawning, especially with the arrival on the scene of rock 'n' roll music and the growing popularity of television.

The BBC's embryonic television service was an early adopter of sans serif lettering (figs 165–6), partly because they were so readily available but also because well-defined edges of the individual letters were easier for the low-resolution cameras and transmission/reception equipment to reproduce. The late-1940s test card (it was literally a piece of card in the early days, later electronically generated)

164

Festival Titling was the official typeface for the Festival of Britain in 1951.

ABCDEFGHIJK
LMNOPQRSTU
VWXYZ123456

TYPE
for
MASSEELEY
HOT PROCESS

"GAMES" SERIES

BOWLS

40 mm.

Bowls

SQUASH

25 mm.

Squash

CRICKET

15 mm.

Cricket

A B C D E F G H I J K L M N O P Q R S T U V W X Y Z
a b c d e f g h i j k l m n o p q r s t u v w x y z

165 (left)

From the mid 1950s, Gill Sans was largely replaced in a number of television captions by Masseeley's Games typeface, a hybrid of Johnston and Gill.

166 (above)

All the early television services in the UK used some Gill Sans. The BBC News rotating animated logo was in Gill Sans Bold Condensed from 1948.

for the television service featured a single letter at the bottom, starting with 'A' (the longest-running being the 'C' card, 1948–64). From the 1940s until the 1980s, when computerisation was introduced, the lettering used was Gill Sans Medium (usually in white). Gill was also used for programme titles, captions, internal memoranda, labels, signage and notepaper and occasionally in *Radio Times* features. This undoubtedly influenced later design decisions by the corporation. During the 1950s a special, condensed typeface was created by a hot-metal typesetter, Masson Seeley (aka "Masseeley'), for television credits (fig.165). Known as the Games series and closely based on Johnston's Omnibus alphabet (fig.168), it was designed to fit more letters onto each line, and only marketed to the BBC and some commercial production companies. When Independent television launched in 1955, it too employed Gill Sans — on most test cards, for instance — as

FOR **PROPERTY LOST**
ON TRAINS, BUSES, TRAMS

Apply **LONDON TRANSPORT
LOST PROPERTY OFFICE**

200 BAKER STREET N.W.1. adjoining Baker Street Station

MONDAY to FRIDAY 10·6   SATURDAY 10·1

When ideas crop up...

...don't keep them to yourself

- Don't wonder why someone else hasn't thought of it.

- If you can see a better way of doing a job, or an improvement to any aspect of our undertaking, tell us about it.

- If an award is granted the least you will get is £1.

- Even if it cannot be used, your idea may still earn you an award if it has been well thought out.

Get Suggestions Forms from your Office, set down your ideas briefly, put them in the envelopes provided and

Send them to the Suggestions Bureau

from here

to **South Bank Exhibition & Royal Festival Hall**

Post 'S' Sticker Here

to Festival **Pleasure Gardens**

Post 'P' Sticker Here

- To Exhibition of Science & Books and London Transport Poster Exhibition Book to SOUTH KENSINGTON STATION

- To Exhibition of Architecture (Lansbury Poplar) Book to ALDGATE EAST STATION thence by bus

- To London Area Art Schools Exhibition Book to HYDE PARK CORNER STATION

- For all information about travel to and from Festival sites and occasions, apply to British Transport Information Centre or Charing Cross London Transport Station or Traffic Enquiry Office London Transport, 55 Broadway, S.W.1. Abbey 1234

Festival of Britain 1951

STATE OCCASIONS

SERVICE OF DEDICATION AT THE OPENING OF FESTIVAL OF BRITAIN
3rd May

Their Majesties the King and Queen will leave Buckingham Palace at 10.35 a.m. and drive in State to St. Paul's Cathedral by way of The Mall, Trafalgar Square, Strand, Fleet Street, and Ludgate Hill arriving at 11 a.m.   At noon the King will broadcast to the nation from the steps of St. Paul's.

The procession will return by the same route leaving St. Paul's at 12.15 p.m.

Nearest Stations: Victoria, St. James's Park, Westminster, Charing Cross, Trafalgar Square, Strand, Temple, Blackfriars, St. Paul's, Mansion House.

STATE VISIT OF THEIR MAJESTIES THE KING & QUEEN OF DENMARK

8th May
The Royal Party will be met at Victoria Station at 3 p.m. by the King and Queen and will drive in State to Buckingham Palace passing through Wilton Road, Victoria Street, Parliament Square, Whitehall, Trafalgar Square and The Mall.   A Guard of Honour at Victoria will be provided by the Coldstream Guards.

Nearest Stations: Victoria, St. James's Park, Westminster, Charing Cross, Trafalgar Square, Strand, Green Park.

10th May
The King and Queen of Denmark will leave Buckingham Palace at noon to drive in State to Guildhall by way of The Mall, Trafalgar Square, Strand, Fleet Street, St. Paul's, Cheapside and King Street. The Honourable Artillery Company will provide a Guard of Honour at Guildhall.

Nearest Stations: Victoria, St. James's Park, Green Park, Trafalgar Square, Strand, Charing Cross, Temple, Aldwych, Blackfriars, St. Paul's, Mansion House, Cannon Street, Bank.

On each occasion the route will be lined by detachments from the three Services.

did BBC Radio, which distributed recordings of programmes as vinyl discs with the title and other lettering set in Gill Sans on the centre label.

Revisions to Johnston

With London Transport nationalised and its range of services and geographical area enlarged, it was inevitable that the amount of accompanying printed material would increase too, and commensurate with that the demands on the fonts of Johnston. By the early 1950s, the Johnston wooden printing type (dating back to the 1920s) was becoming worn out. This, and perhaps a drive to modernise, further pushed commercial artists and the LT publicity department to seek alternative typefaces for at least some of its printed material. It is from this point that the balance shifted away from Johnston, with increasing reliance placed by London Transport on Gill Sans and other typefaces (fig.167).

At the same time, Johnston for the purposes of signage underwent further revision. An updated version of the *Standard Signs* manual was produced in 1954 with several key changes, one of which was to permit the limited return of the word 'UNDERGROUND' in certain circumstances. Although not specified in the guidelines, there were also two minor revisions to the Johnson lettering. The first was initiated by the lighting department, which needed to develop a version that did not flare, as the original letters had done, when lit from behind inside the

167 (opposite)

The loss of Johnston on London Transport (LT) publicity began almost as soon as peace was declared. A 1946 lost property poster (top left) relies mostly on Gill Sans for its message, as does a 1950 poster eliciting ideas from LT staff (top right). It's impossible to find any Johnston on the Festival of Britain posters from 1951 (bottom left) and again Gill Sans dominates on a poster for 'State Occasions' (bottom right).

168

Johnston's bus blind lettering was revised again in the late 1950s to be more legible when set on a black background.

Railway publicity was virtually all set in Gill Sans from almost as soon as nationalisation happened: a relatively simple task considering how ubiquitous the typeface was in virtually every major printer in the UK. Here: Golden Arrow leaflet from 1950 (left); and a steamer tour of Scotland from 1957 (right).

illuminated light boxes, commonly used for signage on the Underground. Later known as Thin, the revised alphabet was only produced in capitals and numerals and only ever utilised on the glass covering of box signs, in frosted white on a black background. Another revision for Johnston also sat on a black background: the extra-condensed, revised version of the Omnibus letter (fig.168).

British Rail modernisation

During the 1950s other sans serifs were coming to the fore and what has become known as the International Typographic Style, or Swiss Style, gained momentum with the release of enormously successful typefaces like Folio, Univers and Neue Haas Grotesk (which later became Helvetica, p.147). A handful of these typefaces crept into British Railways publicity as it continued to modernise, with the conversion of many routes to diesel or electric. The nationwide roll-out of Gill Sans lettering on signs (which had begun in 1948) was still ongoing, slowly expunging much of the original Victorian and Edwardian lettering. Gill Sans of course also still featured on the bulk of publicity material (fig.169), although not without negative connotations as it became synonymous with the posters announcing the closure of branch lines from the mid 1950s.

Charting new territories

The Ordnance Survey (OS) had begun experimenting with phototypesetting as far back as 1949. It also chose to introduce more sans seriffed lettering into its

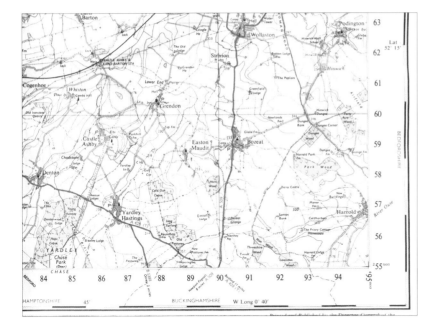

The corner of this Ordnance Survey map from 1953 shows the mixture of Times New Roman for village names and Gill Sans for farms and woods, etc., and in the borders for counties.

maps – Gill Sans, once again. As cartography historian Richard Oliver explains: 'The standard design for the 7th Series (only introduced after the first 38 of the 190 sheets had been produced) mixed Times New Roman with Gill Sans. I can't recall the use of Gill Sans on any OS mapping before 1950–51' (fig.170). The mixture of lettering was continued on other small-scale maps produced in the 1950s and 1960s. The reason for the introduction of Gill Sans is not known but, as Oliver says, it would certainly stand out from other forms of labelling on a map.[3]

Not just maps but school books, especially atlases, began to be set in Gill Sans during the 1950s, firming up in the minds of millions of children the typeface's association with officialdom. The typeface had more glamorous associations too. This was the decade when air travel became much more accessible and the jet age was dawning. British Overseas Airways Corporation (BOAC) began its first non-stop transatlantic de Havilland Comet jet flights in 1958, marking the start of a new epoch in air travel. The company heavily promoted its new routes with maps – all set in Gill Sans – that made globetrotting seem easy.

Spreading the word

As Britain was forced to modernise, one area remained creakingly outdated: the nation's telephone numbering. Subscriber Trunk Dialling, a system that still exists, began in Bristol during 1958, but in the UK's five biggest cities – London, Birmingham, Glasgow, Liverpool and Manchester – catchy modern advertising was still quoting phone numbers as a series of letters and numbers (fig.171),

171

Advertising, even in Gill Sans, was plagued by Britain's anachronistic telephone system. A shipping advert from 1955 has its central London telephone number displayed in letters and digits.

such as the celebrated WHItehall 1212, the phone number of Scotland Yard,
former headquarters of London's Metropolitan Police. Other countries had
dispensed with their archaic schemes, so with the introduction of international
direct dialling, the possibility for incorrect routing arose. Britain's six biggest
cities (Edinburgh was added to the list) were obliged to change to all-figure
dialling from 1966 and this huge job necessitated a torrent of publicity to be
unleashed upon the country, much of it in the Post Office's Gill Sans.

Gill Sans was the default typeface for other official printed ephemera too.
Government publications were issued through Her Majesty's Stationary Office
(HMSO). Continuing a trend started in wartime, the department embraced Gill
Sans as its in-house typeface. They produced a number of books and guidelines
on how to employ the lettering (fig.172), further cementing the link between
the typeface and authority.

Outside the capital, it was probably the most widely used typeface family for
public transport. Serif lettering was rarely employed. Tram and bus operators
were forced to produce millions of pieces of printed information for passengers
and, given that Gill Sans was now so widely available, it was inevitable that
(perhaps unless otherwise specified by the operators) it was co-opted nationally

Univers and Helvetica

By the late 1940s and early 1950s, sans serifs had become hugely popular. Following their successful implementation for hot-metal typesetting, the creation of Gill Sans and their dominance in the market, one of the next biggest arrivals was Univers (fig.174). Young Swiss type-designer Adrian Frutiger (1928–2015) was employed by the Paris-based foundry Deberny et Peignot to prepare typefaces for transfer from the older Linotype system to the cutting-edge technology of the period: phototypesetting. Charles Peignot, who had foreseen the need for a unified font family, asked Frutiger to design something similar to Futura (p.122), but disliking the appearance of the Geometrics, Frutiger preferred to work on updating a Neo-Grotesque and took Akzidenz-Grotesk (p.28) as his starting point. Between 1954 and the release of the typeface in 1957, he constructed 21 variants of Univers, numbering each weight progressively (from 3 for the lightest to 8 for the heaviest).

The release of Univers in 1957 coincided with the work of Max Miedinger on another Neo-Grotesque, also loosely based on Akzidenz, that he at first called Neue Haas Grotesk. Stempel, the parent company of the foundry Miedinger worked for, changed the name to Helvetica in 1960. The story of this face is the subject of many books, papers and articles – and even a 2007 film[4] – and it has risen to become one of the most widely used sans serifs of all time. Helvetica has also spawned several clones and derivatives: produced in 1982 by Robin Nicholas of Monotype, Arial was designed with the home computer in mind. Nicholas freely admits it was intended to be 'bland' and also that despite its requirements to follow the shape of Helvetica's letters, certain letters, like the upper-case 'R' and 'G' and the lower-case 'r', owe much to the structure of Gill Sans which, arguably, is used more in the UK at least than Helvetica or Univers.[5]

174

The cover of Deberny et Peignot's 1960 catalogue (top), to showcase the entire Univers family. Further variants were made, including, in 1973, a specially commissioned version of Univers capitals to be used exclusively by the Paris Métro. After Toronto Rapid Transit (1954) and the Mexico City Metro (1968), this was the most widespread use of a specific typeface created for transport since Johnston for the London Underground. New York City Subway (above) migrated from Akzidenz-Grotesk to Helvetica around 1989.

PLEASE AVOID THE RUSH HOURS 08 30-09 30, 16 30-18 00

MOST WEST-END STATIONS
ARE OPEN UNTIL 12.30 A.M.
(11.30 P.M. ON SUNDAYS)

**CHEAP
EVENING RETURN
TICKETS TO TOWN**

by Underground
ASK AT THE TICKET OFFICE

FROM HERE Every day.
The first 'cheap' train is at the following times:
Mondays to Fridays (Thursdays)
Saturdays and at   on Sundays.

Alterations to tram and bus stops in Argyle Street and Dumbarton Road

Commencing on **SUNDAY, 3rd JUNE 1962,** the position of some tram and bus stops in Argyle Street and Dumbarton Road will be altered.

44 BATH STREET,
GLASGOW, C.2.

 CORPORATION · TRANSPORT

E. R. L. FITZPAYNE,
General Manager.

GLASGOW
CORPORATION
TRANSPORT

70 YEARS OF TRAVELLING BY **UNDERGROUND** IN **GLASGOW**

**14th DECEMBER 1896
14th DECEMBER 1966**

ACQUIRED BY CORPORATION 1923   ELECTRIFIED 1935

A SELECTION OF UNDERGROUND PHOTOGRAPHS ON VIEW AT MUSEUM OF TRANSPORT, ALBERT DRIVE

175 (left and top)
—
Spot the Johnston? Throughout the 1960s, Johnston gave further ground to Gill Sans in London Transport publicity, as can be seen in these posters: *Cheap Evening Return Tickets to Town* by Victor Galbraith, from 1962, and *Please Avoid the Rush Hours* from 1966.

176 (above and centre)
—
Although Johnston was not permitted for use outside London Transport, Gill Sans certainly was and public transportation organisations embraced the typeface. Here examples from Glasgow Corporation tram services (1962) and the city's Subway (1966).

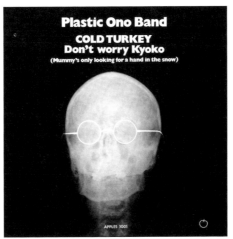

177 (far left)

Manufactured by Solari Udine of Italy,
split flap displays were a common sight in
stations and airports. Most used Gill Sans
letters.

178 (left)

The sleeve cover for the Plastic Ono
Band's single 'Cold Turkey' (1969) was the
first to be designed by John Kosh.

for myriad applications throughout the second half of the twentieth century
(figs 175–6).

Top of the types

One of the most regular outings for Gill Sans from the latter half of the
twentieth century has been on vinyl record sleeves. Many graphic designers
were inspired by it, including London-born designer (John) Kosh, who has used
the typeface on scores of classic album covers throughout his career, for hugely
popular bands from The Beatles to The Who. As Kosh explains:

> Using Gill Sans was the most natural choice in the world for me having
> grown up in east London surrounded by all those red buses with Johnston
> lettering and Gill Sans on everything else. If I could have used Johnston I
> would have, but the closest available was Gill. It's so clear and legible; Gill
> Sans is like a hero to me.[6]

He first used Gill Extra Bold on Apple Records' 'Cold Turkey' cover (Plastic
Ono Band, 1969, fig.178) and carried it through *Abbey Road* (1969, back cover
in Gill Sans), *Let It Be* (1970) in Gill Extra Bold; ELO's *Out of the Blue* (1977) in
Gill Sans Bold; *Eagles Greatest Hits, Vol.2* (1982) in Gill Sans Cameo; and many
hundreds more.

Johnston lags behind

The dominance of Gill Sans was in direct contrast to the marginalisation of
Johnston: despite revision to the typeface the problem continued to be its
limited range of weights and sizes. From the late 1960s, for almost a decade,

Kinneir and Calvert: the heirs to Johnston

ABCDEFGH
IJKLMNOP
QRSTUVW
XYZ. 123
4567890

179 (above)

This slightly condensed sans serif, with a passing resemblance to Johnston, was issued in the 1940s for use on Britain's road signage. Leading up to the 1950s, this was a bit of a mess as local authorities, responsible for the highways, were not compelled to conform to international guidelines evolved since the 1920s.

By the late 1950s Britain was in need of new road signage. Existing signs from the 1940s were set in sans serif capitals (fig.179), but they didn't comply with international standards and the first new motorway was about to open. The job fell to a pair who proved to be the most influential British sans serif typeface designers since Johnston and Gill.

Typographer and graphic designer Richard ('Jock') Kinneir (1917–94) joined the Design Research Unit (DRU) consultancy in 1949 before opening his own practice in 1956. He also taught part time at the Chelsea School of Art, where he became impressed by the work of student Margaret Calvert (b.1936). Kinneir took her on as an assistant to help him with his first commission: the signage for the Yorke, Rosenberg and Mardall rebuild at Gatwick Airport. The resulting design – black sans serifs on a yellow background – was to set the standard for airport way finding for decades (fig.180).

Kinneir and Calvert were then appointed by a committee, led by Sir Colin Anderson, to look at new motorway lettering. Meticulous in their research, they assessed how letters would be viewed from a car, discovering, in their investigations, that the maximum angle at which a driver could safely switch their gaze from the road to a sign was about 15 degrees and that it took about four seconds to process information when travelling at an average of 70mph (110kph). The pair also concluded that lettering in capitals alone would be more difficult to absorb at speed than a mixture of upper- and lower-case letters.

Taking all this into consideration, but ignoring Anderson's advice not to create a new typeface, Kinneir and Calvert designed a sans serif that they believed would suit the British landscape, one they based loosely on Akzidenz-Grotesk (p.28). They borrowed the lower-case 'l' from Johnston (p.53) but made the

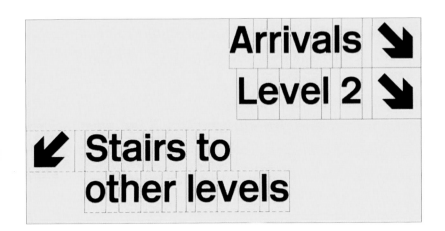

180 (left and below)

Calvert and Kinneir's black upper- and lower-case sans serif on a yellow background (left) was adopted for the renovation of Gatwick Airport (1956–8). Comparison of the 1940s alphabet (below) with Kindersley's (in the centre) to Kinneir and Calvert's clean modern upper- and lower-case sans serif. Gill Sans was also considered (second from bottom) but the Transport alphabet (bottom) became the familiar face of British roads.

curves more steeply angled to aid visibility when the lettering was viewed at night under car headlights. They also designed a set of condensed numerals for the road numbers and some key letters for road classifications and compass points. Full-size signs were mocked up and placed along the first stretch of new motorway (Preston bypass) before its opening in 1958. Its success led to Kinneir and Calvert's alphabet, Transport (fig.180), being adopted across the motorway network – a form of lettering that is still in use on British road signs today.

A one-time pupil of Eric Gill, David Kindersley, having seen the signs before they were rolled out across the whole network, denigrated them as looking as though 'designed by lunatic drivers'.[7] He had been working on his own slab-seriffed all-caps alphabet (MoT Serif) and a public debate forced a comparison between Kinneir and Calvert's lettering and Kindersley's. The vote came down on the side of the Transport alphabet, whose more modern look was preferred. A second committee, formed under Sir Walter Worboys, examined remaining non-motorway signage. Various letterforms were tested, including Kindersley's, Gill Sans Condensed and Transport, but following testing at the Road Research Laboratory, the Transport typeface won.

The success of Kinneir and Calvert's sans serif secured them other pivotal projects, including an overhaul of British Railways. Since 1948 Gill Sans had been used, but following moves to modernise, the DRU was commissioned in 1964 to address signage, with Kinneir and Calvert working on the lettering. Creating another new typeface – this one to be read at a more leisurely speed, by

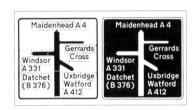

Basic Elements				
Rail alphabet black letters		sheet no.	1/11	
		issued	Apr 1965	

For notes on the use of this alphabet refer to Sheet 1/10.

181

Derived from the Airport lettering, Kinneir and Calvert's 1965 Rail Alphabet differed subtly from their road network version. Calvert wanted to create something quite bland-looking, as if no one had designed it. The alphabet was also adopted by the Danish state rail operator DSB.

pedestrians – they kept with the sans serif look for their Rail Alphabet (fig.181). This, along with the DRU's iconic double-arrow logo and a name change to British Rail, was included in a comprehensive new corporate-identity manual, first issued in 1965.

The success of Rail Alphabet inspired the Department of Health and Social Security, which was looking for a unified typeface for the National Health Service. Calvert returned to the Airport and Rail alphabets, refining them for the introduction of modular signage systems, and it was adopted by the NHS in the early 1970s. Kinneir and Calvert have made some of the most outstanding contributions to sans serifs in the UK since Johnston and Gill.

the much-cherished Johnston lettering appeared less than 20 times among hundreds of LT posters produced by external design agencies.

The advent of rub-down, dry transfer lettering introduced in the late 1950s had helped Johnston to some extent. Growing in popularity in the 1960s, first with the technical drawing and architectural professions and progressively with graphic designers, by the 1970s it had even been introduced to the general public, with special packs for kids. One of the biggest brands, Letraset, whose three most popular families of typefaces were Gill Sans (fig.182), Helvetica and Univers. Another manufacturer was Rapitype, which also produced a version of Johnston exclusively for the use of LT, and this greatly helped designers to continue to use the typeface in different sizes, especially for display work where close spacing was preferred. It wasn't a complete solution, however, as the process was fiddly and time consuming.

Johnston was now behind the times. It was tricky for agencies to reproduce wood letter and metal type shapes for phototypesetting. At the same time, Gill Sans was becoming universally used for all LT's smaller point sizes. Tim Demuth, who sat on London Transport's design committee, recalls how one agency (Foote Cone & Belding), were 'allowed more freedom and attacked the Johnston lettering as being antiquated and ready for replacement. They were making much use of Franklin Gothic for headlines (fig.183) and Bookman for text, all centred and closely spaced in their campaigns, and they brought this into their work for LT'.[8]

Custom-made corporate typefaces were virtually unknown at this stage: faces were then, as now, developed, promoted and updated by foundries, so LT's insistence on an exclusive typeface, with just two weights, became a burden, as typesetting technology evolved. However, there was the Thin version of Johnston created to illuminate signs and there was also an italic drawn by Berthold Wolpe (1905–89). The German type-designer had met Morison in 1932 and was commissioned by Monotype to produce a seriffed typeface, Albertus (titling capitals by 1935, full range by 1940). He designed a number of dust jackets for the Gollancz series between 1935 and 1945 (which included some use of Gill Sans, especially Gill Kayo) and, after a spell during the war in an Australian internment camp to which he had been sent with other German nationals living in England, he joined Faber and Faber in 1941 after having been allowed back into Britain. A talented calligrapher and type-designer, Wolpe was asked to redesign the masthead for *The Times*, the

182

Gill Sans Letraset sheet and Rapitype Johnston for London Transport.

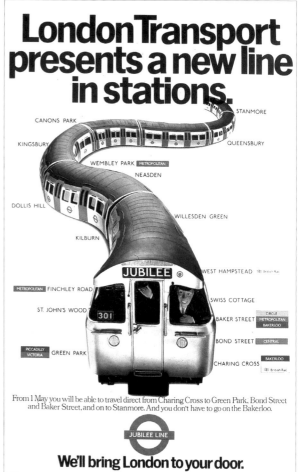

Two posters produced by Foote, Cone & Belding for London Transport. Looking more like an advert for *Time Out* (the London listings magazine which used a similar style), the first (1970), extolling the virtues of the Underground over parking meters, is bereft of Johnston. In the second (1979), only a nod to Johnston is permitted in the destination blind and station/line names on advertising for the new Jubilee line.

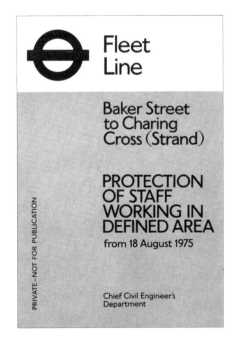

revamped lettering first appearing in 1966. In 1972 he was commissioned by LT to design an italic for the Johnston type family (fig.184).

Another attempt to tidy up some of Johnston's worn-out letters was made by Walter Tracy (1914–95), an unsung hero of the story. He had a hand in *The Times* too, updating the newspaper's own serif from Times New Roman to Times Europa in 1972. Tracy made adjustments to Johnston's lower-case 'a', 'g', 'l', 'r', 'w' and 'y', and his revised lettering was used to a limited extent – and certainly more widely than Wolpe's italic – particularly by Demuth, who incorporated it on several posters and maps between 1973 and 1978.

The challenge was that it was still very difficult to adapt Johnston to modern cold typesetting, in which a minimum of three or four weights were needed. Two of the biggest drivers to improve (or jettison altogether) Johnston were the extension of the Piccadilly line to Heathrow (due in 1977) and the forthcoming Fleet line (fig.184). Acutely aware of Johnston's limitations in a more sophisticated age, LT staff like Demuth and the design committee hoped that the typeface could be modernised in time for these big events, but that proved unrealistic. The organisation was not able to deliver two new sections of Underground line and carry out a radical overhaul of its flagship lettering all at the same time. Despite the fact that the first new section of the Tube since the 1960s had opened without the benefit of new lettering for its signage, work was afoot to shake things up radically in the next decade.

184
_____

A Fleet line in-house booklet from 1975 (top left) employs Granby. Demuth redesigned the *Night Buses* guide from extensive use of Gill Sans (1971, top centre) to incorporating Tracy's Johnston (1973, top right). Wolpe's Johnston Italic (bottom right), designed in 1973, was not used much.

HAÇIENDA

FAC 51 MAY 21 I YEAR

8

New Johnston and Gill Nova 1980–present

The 1980s may not be remembered as the most stylish decade, but for the Johnston lettering it was a time of rebirth, and Gill Sans began to shake off its associations with post-war austerity. (Indeed, it was increasingly prevalent in popular culture, figs 185 and 188.) The Jubilee line had opened in 1979 without any updating of typography – but the seeds of what was to happen to the Johnston alphabet in the 1980s were already being sown in the dying days of the previous decade.

The London Transport design committee was aware of the lack of a modern recut of Johnston on film (everything up until Walter Tracy's 1974 refinements had essentially sprung from Johnston's original drawings in post-Edwardian times) and it was some observations by Tracy in 1975 and June 1979 on the difficulties of using the existing inflexible fonts that may have nudged the committee into action. In a letter to publicity officer Michael Levey, he suggested it would be comparatively easy and inexpensive to produce a film or font for modern phototypesetting.[1] Conscious of the need for immediate action, the design committee, chaired by Donald Hall, the director of architecture and design, responded with uncharacteristic haste. After

185 (opposite)

Peter Saville produced the identity and the first anniversary poster for Manchester's Haçienda nightclub in 1983. The industrial look of 'FAC 51' had already been set by its architect Ben Kelly. Saville revealed that the cedilla of Gill's 'Ç' followed by the letter 'I' loosely resembled the Haçienda club's 'FAC' number, '51' – essentially guaranteeing that no other typeface was ever in the running but Gill Sans.

I. Original Johnston Range:

There are six variations but only medium and bold romans are available for LT's general printed publicity.

ABCDEFGHIJKLMNOPQRSTUVWXYZ& ;:!?''()
£1234567890

Original Johnston Bold (no l.c. available): attributed to Johnston but in fact drawn by Charles Pickering when an apprentice at Baynard Press. Johnston would have done it by himself but was sent the drawings for his comments; he disagreed on the proportion of thickness of stroke to cap height.

ABCDEFGHIJKLMNOPQRSTUVWXYZ& .;!? ()
abcdefghijklmnopqrstuvwxyz £1234567890

Original Johnston Medium: the standard face. Some letters were subsequently redrawn by Walter Tracey. Only these two (Med & Bold) are available for LT's printed publicity. Available as metal type and on film, and as dry transfer sheet.

ABCDEFGHIJKLMNOPQRSTUVWXYZ&
abcdefghijklmnopqrstuvwxyz 1234567890 1234567890

Original Johnston Light: provenance unknown. Not normally available, except for signing when fluorescent lamps are used. Available only on film. Two weights for figures.

ABCDEFGHIJKLMNOPQRSTUVWXYZ& ()
1234567890

Original Johnston Bold Condensed: provenance unknown.

ABCDEFGHIJKLMNOPQRSTUVWXYZ&
abcdefghijklmnopqrstuvwxyz 1234567890 4

Original Johnston Medium Condensed: Christian Barman attributes this to Johnston, but I (Colin Banks) seem to remember that Harry Carter was saying some years ago that he had drawn at least figures in the 30's. These condensed faces (Med & Bold) are available only on film, and designed specifically for use on bus blinds (destination panels).

ABCDEFGHIJKLMNOPQRSTUVWXYZ& :;!?
abcdefghijklmnopqrstuvwxyz£1234567890

Original Johnston Medium Italic: the italic was drawn in comparatively recent times by Berthold Wolpe, but not cut. At present, available only on film.

Eiichi Kono
at Banks & Miles April 1980

186 (above)

Kono's assembly of all previous versions of Johnston's alphabet gave a total of just six, some of which, like Wolpe's italic, had effectively never been used.

187 (left)

Colin Banks's initial sketches, would have taken Johnston in a very different direction. In places it is positively heretical: the 'g' is clearly too wide and the capital 'S' looks as though it might have come straight from Akzidenz-Grotesk. His lower-case 's' and upper-case 'C' seem oddly off course, too.

briefly considering Kinneir and Calvert for the job, and also Tracy himself, LT's Basil Hooper commissioned progressive graphic design agency Banks and Miles (B&M, also responsible for a double-line alphabet for the Post Office, p.172) to appraise the Johnston lettering and propose modern alternatives. According to Dutch designer Jim Jansen, both News Gothic Bold Condensed and Univers Bold were discussed by the team as potential replacements.[2] By 28 June 1979, B&M had conducted an initial assessment, taking these proposals into consideration but concluding that to lose Johnston could diminish LT's heritage. On 2 July, Tim Demuth had presented a summary and timetable to the LT board, who commissioned a trial bold, regular, italic and narrow version of Johnston from B&M.

Kono resuscitates Johnston

B&M's co-founder, Colin Banks, was of a similar opinion to other contemporary agencies in believing that the days of an alphabet created in 1916 must be numbered. Banks attempted his own reworking of some letters, evoking typefaces like Helvetica and Univers (fig.187), before passing the job of assessing the range of Johnston to the company's newest recruit, Japanese-born Eiichi Kono. He had worked at first in Japan, generating and managing publicity for German and American optics companies in Tokyo, but, having become fascinated by western typography, he relocated in 1974 to London, where he spent five years at the London College of Printing while also studying graphic information and legibility in print at the Royal College of Art. Kono recalls how on his first day at B&M he was presented with every variation of Johnston that LT had been able to unearth; he then made a visual with his notes on provenance and usage (fig.186).[3]

LT had initially asked for extensions to just two of the existing Johnston weights, regular and bold. Kono recommended attention be focused on designing a new weight, medium, which would sit between the existing regular and bold, providing the most versatile weight for all uses. In his words: 'Doing this would require a completely new approach: "reworking" – instead of "revisioning" of particular letterforms through extrapolation.'[4] Not just tweaking, Kono was proposing a more fundamental rethink of Johnston's proportions:

> Things in a design office were different then. No computers, not even a photocopier at B&M, so I picked up a pencil and a Rotring pen. There was a

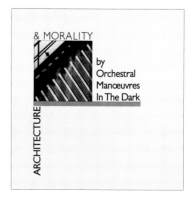

188

Saville also co-founded Manchester's Factory Records in 1978 with Tony Wilson. He used Gill Sans first on The Distractions' 'Time Goes By So Slow' (Fac12, September 1979). He also employed it for Orchestral Manoeuvres in the Dark's 'Red Frame/White Light' (Din6, February 1980) and their first album (also 1980). For OMD's third album, *Architecture & Morality* (DID12), Saville used Medium and Light Gill Sans on the cover in 1981. Neville Brody also employed it for the redesign of *City Limits* magazine (below).

189

Kono's second draft for the medium
(24 July 1979, top), light (August, middle)
and condensed (September, bottom)
demonstrate a razor-sharp appreciation
of Johnston's original intentions
combined with a sense of the spacing
and proportions required in modern
typesetting.

darkroom with an enlarger, and I managed to produce the first presentation
to LT within three weeks, in July 1979, with this proposal to completely
revise and extend the Johnston typeface to three weights. This involved
pencil drawings: re-forming the letters of the broadsheet on tracing paper,
inking, photographing, overlaying sample words, comparing, adjusting,
redrawing, inking, photographing, and so on. I knew this was no way to
produce convincing precise new characters in different sizes, so I demanded
a Photo Mechanical Transfer [PMT] machine. It arrived mid August, and I
was then able to produce incomparably better-quality specimens, and by
the end of September there had been several presentations.[5]

In October 1979, LT gave the go-ahead for the three proposed weights
(fig.189). Kono remembers that even at this stage LT was still not entirely sure
what it wanted: 'What evolved into New Johnston was not necessarily intended
to be the final solution, but due to the lack of time available that is how I
proceeded. I had redrawn every letter by hand, and for me the result was a bit
like a new conductor playing [sic] a different, modern orchestra.'[6]

According to Demuth, B&M deliberately designed a bold condensed (that
was not in the original brief) specifically to compete with the weight of the
Franklin Gothic Bold Condensed then being promoted by agencies like Foote,
Cone & Belding (p.153), as well as a medium and light condensed (but it was not
as condensed as that used on the original bus blinds).[7] Playing down his role,
Demuth continued:

I was only involved at the very end after Kono presented his designs.
Production as letterpress display type was out of the question: the spacing
[involved in] setting individual characters from film or rub-down lettering
[Rapitype] depended too much on the person applying it. So I was already
looking towards keyboard [computerised] setting, knowing that sizes could
extend from 5pt to that needed for large signboards. There would then be
scope for tabular settings, with a keyboard Johnston replacing Gill Sans on
timetables. That is why I got Eiichi to ensure figures were the same width
(including the numeral 1 which he widened by adding the 'tick' similar to
that used on Helvetica, Futura and Granby).[8]

ABCDEFGH
IJKLMNOP*
QRSTUV?!()
WXYZ&£:;

abbcdefgghi
jkllmnopqrr
satuvwxyyz
12344567890

190 (left)

Kono's Photo Mechanical Transfers (PMTs) of the medium weight – capitals and lower case, dating from around mid January 1980.

191 (below)

By March 1980 Kono's PMTs had been transferred to film; here he holds the original film for a medium 'U' and bold 'B' at the London Transport Museum (photo taken in 2015).

A comparison sheet made in 2016 by Kono illustrating the differences and similarities between his designs and the originals.

Once the new lettering had been completed and signed off by the design committee, Demuth then sent the New Johnston letters to a London-based company, Star Illustration, for high-resolution photographic scanning and transferring onto 35mm filmstrips that were then distributed to all authorised studios and printers (fig.191). Digitisation and unitisation (calculating the space between each and every letter) was carried out by a company at Princes Risborough in conjunction with the Setting Room in Tonbridge and the type foundry H. Berthold AG in West Berlin.

The adoption of New Johnston

The first weights of New Johnston became available in mid 1980, when a handful of trial leaflets and posters were produced (fig.193). By the summer of that year, they had been fully approved, but the process of hand drawing every glyph for each weight, transferring to film and distributing to the regular printers took months. Nevertheless, enthusiastic LT staff like Demuth and Chris Leadbetter were making use of as many variants as possible. It is no exaggeration to say that Kono's efforts saved the day for Johnston's alphabet despite some purist's reservations about spacing. Although it is likely that Johnston lettering would have survived on station signs and logos (the bull's-eyes, now known as roundels), had it not been for Kono's modernisation of the typeface, LT would have moved permanently away from it – on printed material at least.

One of the earliest outings for the revised typeface was in 1981 as part of the 'Fares Fair' campaign in which the Greater London Council (GLC), under its leader Ken Livingstone, reduced Tube and bus ticket prices. The scheme was eventually outlawed by the Thatcher government, but not before reams of printed material, set mostly in New Johnston, were distributed to Londoners (fig.194). Once the government had stopped the GLC from subsidising ticket prices, a public campaign, at arm's length from LT, then ensued under the banner 'Keep Fares Fair', with stickers and fliers produced in Gill Sans. A touch of irony, perhaps, in seeing the two 'faces' of authority both flying in the face of authority.

Although the creation of the full range of nine fonts in three weights took until the late 1980s, with a version for setting body text, 'New Johnston Book', not arriving until 1991, New Johnston was nevertheless widely applied throughout the London Transport network. This took place as part of a general refurbishment since a large number of stations and vehicles had barely seen had a lick of paint, let alone any new signage, since before the war. A series of Underground station refits during the 1980s was able to utilise New Johnston to great effect (fig.195).

A unified look for Underground signage

While the revised typeface helped rejuvenate the look of Underground stations and buses, application of the lettering throughout the 1980s was deemed somewhat haphazard. To address this issue, LT design manager Roger Hughes commissioned a signage report from the brand consultancy Henrion Ludlow Schmidt (HLS). Published in 1984, the report recommended a fundamental overhaul of signage.[9] HLS immediately grasped the significance and strengths of New Johnston, focusing on how it would best be displayed (fig.196). They proposed that only station name

New fares on London Buses
STARTING 24 FEBRUARY

BUSES 114, 136, 182, 183, 186, 209, 258, 286

There will be a general fares increase on London Transport buses.

To speed up the one-man-operated buses, these services will change to a flat-fare system - a fare of 20p (child 8p) will apply for any journey.*

*On bus 258 the flat fare will only apply for any journey wholly within the Borough of Harrow, otherwise standard fares will continue to be charged.

193

'New fares on London Buses' is a mock-up from 1982 that also uses the condensed version of New Johnston.

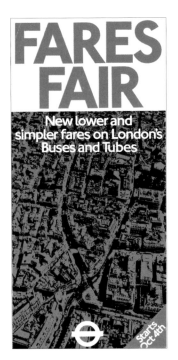

194 (left)

The 1981 'Fares Fair' policy gave rise to masses of publicity in New Johnston, such as this pamphlet (far left) from the time. The campaign to keep the Fares Fair was all set in Gill Sans as this 1982 flier (left) shows.

195 (left and centre)

The major rebuild in the 1980s to join Strand and Trafalgar Square into one new interchange station called 'Charing Cross' allowed New Johnston to be used on Bakerloo friezes. At Heathrow Terminal 4 station (opened in 1986) an enlarged name frieze was installed. Because of the size of the letters, this had to be executed by hand.

Pages from the Henrion Ludlow Schmidt report on signage of 1984 showing how New Johnston was to be used. The first image (top) shows how not to apply messages, next, a proposal of how tunnels would look with the new signage (second row); friezes and roundels in the new lettering (bottom three).

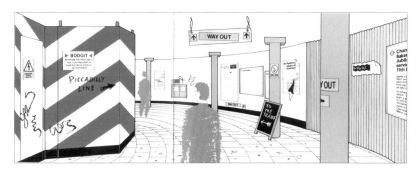

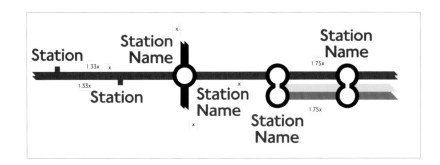

Such was the meticulous attention to detail that even the placing of station names on the map was stipulated precisely by Henrion Ludlow Schmidt.

198 (below)

The Tyne-Wear Metro typeface was created by Margaret Calvert in 1980 – the first major transit system using serifs (top). Docklands Light Rail adopted a similar block serif for lettering in 1987 (second and third rows). In 1991 Docklands shifted to Frutiger (fourth row) and all signs were replaced (bottom). The move didn't last long: New Johnston was rolled out in the 2000s and the non-adoption of Johnston from the outset is now seen as a bit of an error.

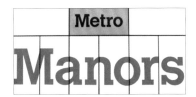

signs, canopy fascias, platform friezes and the roundel itself be in capitals. The lettering for all other signage should now appear in upper and lower case – a radical change since up until this time it had mostly been in capital letters. Signage was to be exclusively in New Johnston Medium; HLS saw no place for Light, Condensed or Italic, apart from use in publicity material.

Their proposals were then implemented by a team under the LT marketing and development director, Dr Henry Fitzhugh. During the process Fitzhugh's team compiled the *London Underground Sign Manual*, which, published in 1989, was revised and reissued many times. The New Johnston typeface was so much of a cornerstone that, along with the roundel and line colours, it was the first item to feature in the book, in a chapter entitled 'Basic Elements'. As stipulated by the manual, all signs were to be simplified to one message per panel and every word not in New Johnston (apart from designated 'heritage' stations) would be replaced. Black glass illuminated signs were ruled out in favour of enamel signs with a white background (except for essential 'Way out' signs). Letter and line spacing was so crucial to the look that it too was specified: the x-height of the station name text had to match the thickness of the coloured line (fig.197). The switch to upper and lower case in 1986, and computer-aided design the following year, also put designers on their mettle.

'Old' Johnston revised

With New Johnston now firmly established and 'old' Johnston permitted only at a limited number of heritage stations, the original typeface was now authorised for use outside London Transport. Its first commercial release was under exclusive licence (by the London Transport Museum in 1997) to P22 Type Foundry in the US. Typographers Richard Kegler and Paul D. Hunt at P22 made some alterations to Johnston's original designs, producing it only in regular and bold capitals to begin with. It was first available to the general public on three floppy disks and included a set of ornaments with borders and the ribbon shapes that could be used for above and below the letters. After a couple

199

For the Diamond Jubilee of London Transport in 1993, a special set of original Johnston Sans 'Trial Proofs' were run off from the surviving wooden type by Ian Mortimer. Lovingly made and exquisitely printed, just 14 numbered sets were produced (four of them on handmade paper) and are now highly sought after.

of years, a different electronic version was designed by Richard Dawson and Dave Farey of the International Typeface Corporation. Released in 1999 as ITC Johnston, with light, medium and bold (in upper and lower case), it added small capitals to the range and correctly proportioned italics and was closer to New Johnston than the P22 version. The issuing of both of these electronic versions helped the Johnston lettering seep out into the public realm.

The BBC updates its logo

London Transport was not the only large institution to consider making revisions to the lettering that embodied it. The BBC's inclined sans serif logo from 1959 had been updated in the 1980s by Michael Peters & Partners, but by the mid 1990s it was looking rather dated alongside the Futura bold condensed italic typeface used on printed material and for some wording on screen. By this stage, the corporation had 180 different logos in use and were conscious of the need to standardise in preparation to keep in tune with the fast-moving digital age. The rebranding was given to Martin Lambie-Nairn, who had designed the Channel 4 logo for its launch in 1982 (fig.201). The BBC had occasionally used Gill Sans for title sequences, test cards and other graphics (p.141), and a handful of shows had featured the typeface too (*Omnibus*, 1982; *Points of View*, 1983; *Panorama*, 1988; *Question Time*, 1994; *Modern Times*, 1996). Lambie-Nairn now proposed to implement it universally.

In his view, the old logo now looked uncomfortable when seen alongside BBC brand names. Adobe's Gill Sans (licensed from Monotype) was perfect

200

Despite the Henrion Ludlow Schmidt report, a change of structure in 1984 resulted in a new name: London Regional Transport. There was no threat to overall design but the logo was not set in Johnston.

TYPEFACES

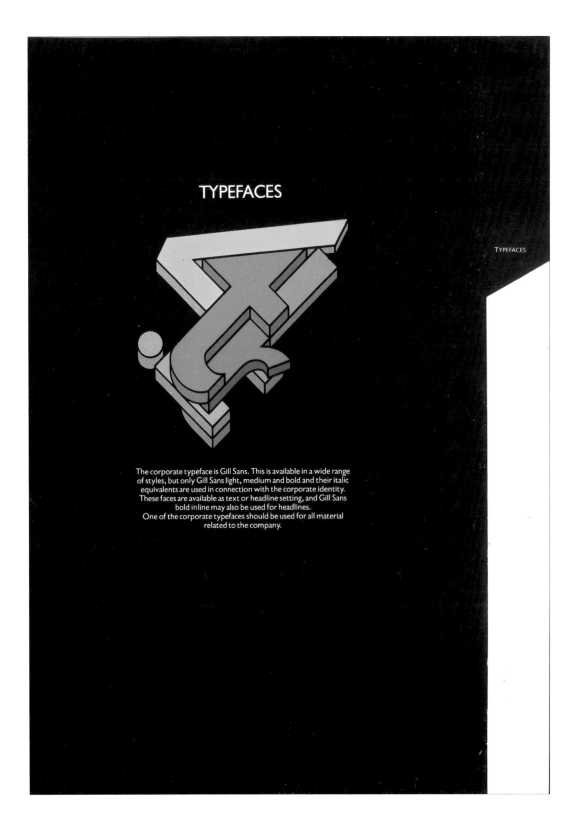

The corporate typeface is Gill Sans. This is available in a wide range of styles, but only Gill Sans light, medium and bold and their italic equivalents are used in connection with the corporate identity. These faces are available as text or headline setting, and Gill Sans bold inline may also be used for headlines.
One of the corporate typefaces should be used for all material related to the company.

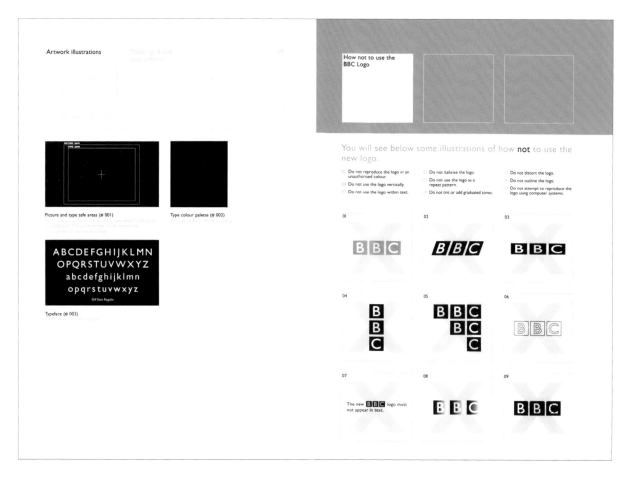

201 (opposite)

The logo for the newly launched Channel 4, 1982. Designed by the Robinson Lambie-Nairn agency, its award-winning graphic style set a new standard for British television. Along with the channel name, guidelines for advertisers and designers and on-screen graphics were all set in Gill Sans Medium for many years. Gill Sans Light was also used for some on-screen programme menus, with Bold on press packs and marketing.

202 (this page)

The revised BBC logo (bottom right) and pages on how to apply it (above) from the design guidelines produced in 1998, not by Lambie-Nairn as expected, but by the design agency Rodney Fitch, which was responsible for way finding and signage at BBC buildings, such as at Television Centre (centre right), now closed.

for the rebranding because of its impartiality: 'even though we designers love it, people feel like it has no character or personality'; it was also particularly appropriate for the BBC, as Gill's work featured on Broadcasting House itself, in the form of his sculpted panels.

> [Gill Sans] has clear, open counters that work well on screen and by keeping the 'B', 'B' and 'C' panels, we kept the equity and heritage but dropped the unnecessary stripes underneath. Individual channels like ONE, TWO or local radio or regional names then followed neatly and carried the intellectual property in things like the Dada-esque 2 of BBC2 or the hot air balloon of BBC1, and by choosing a typeface that has stood the test of time we avoided the trap of [using] one that might go out of fashion.[10]

For a public broadcasting company there were financial considerations too, as voiced by BBC director Colin Browne in a memo of 1998: 'Research showed that large sections of the audience did not understand that the programmes they enjoyed were produced by the BBC and funded by the licence fee. The greater simplicity of the logo, a reduction in the number of colours and its ease of application on screen will mean significant savings.'[11] It was new signage (at 500 sites across the world) that cost the lion's share of the £5m rebranding expenses, but Lambie-Nairn's work saved the corporation a great deal more than that – money that could be directed at core programming instead.

The BBC's adoption of Gill Sans was a milestone in its post-war comeback, not just because this would raise its profile enormously, but because this gave affirmation of the typeface as more than the face of authority – the epitome of Britishness. As Patrick Cramsie, author of *The Story of Graphic Design* (2010), explained to historian Stephen Skelton, there are strong national preferences for particular typefaces: 'I'm sure the BBC were persuaded to use Gill Sans partly because "a British institution should use a British typeface".'[12]

The battle to keep Johnston

In the long-running saga of transport management in the capital, a new government body emerged in 2000: Transport for London (TfL). It did not initially control the Underground (the government was finalising the transference

203

Pages from the 2003 *Standard Signs* manual featuring the roundel family and 'TfL Johnston' (second row); an incorrectly implemented version at a 2006 rebuild of Euston Square, where the wrong lettering, Gill Sans Bold, appeared on the roundel (top left); temporary vinyl stickers were applied in Arial (top right) at Silverlink Metro stations when they were taken over by the Overground in 2007; Tramlink became the first London Transport mode to utilise the italic New Johnston (2000) with a stylised flash over the initial 'T' (bottom right). (This was all undone in 2003 when new guidelines forced the system to be brought in line with the rest of TfL. Signs that had only been up for three years were replaced.)

of funding of the Underground to public–private partnership, PPP) but assumed responsibility for highways, including taxi licensing. A new corporate identity was needed but the design team had a more urgent matter on their hands: New Johnston would not function on TfL's new computer-operating system. Only two designers, Innes Ferguson and Mo Oshodi, had transferred from the previous set-up and they were trying to find a solution. It would either have to be (expensively) converted or another typeface substituted, they concluded. Monotype was lined up to modernise the typeface, but at the last moment the purchase order was turned down by senior TfL managers – Oshodi recalls being told it was a waste of money and they should make do with Arial.[13] But when the design team was moved from the finance department to advertising, the updating of New Johnston was given the go-ahead, providing the revision included a tick at the top of the numeral '1' to distinguish it from other glyphs. Each letter also needed to be readable for visually impaired people. As even ITC Johnston (used internally at this stage) was not appropriate, the revised face in Monotype's OpenType format was christened TfL Johnston and included a specially constructed new glyph: the roundel. Oshodi and Ferguson immediately incorporated TfL Johnston into a revised edition of the *Standard Signs* manual (issued 2003, fig.203), with an improved family of roundels for each mode of transport, including street management.

Gill and Johnston
on the money

The new Post Office logo with lettering in Gill Sans (bottom). An inline bold (above), based loosely on Gill Sans, was used for main signage, such as here in the Yorkshire village of Ovenden (no relation), before rebranding in the early 1990s.

Given that the GPO was an early adopter of Gill Sans (p.121), it is surprising how few postage stamps featured it. The postal heritage website refers to Gill Sans being tried on 'essays' (preliminary artworks) between 1934 and 1936, but the sans serif was excluded from the finished versions.[14] The range of other typefaces used over the years, from serifs to sans, did not include Gill, an omission that was not rectified until 1985 when a set of commemorative stamps celebrating great British trains was published. In 1986 Gill Sans Extra Condensed was used on a set of Industry Year stamps, and later that year for the Commonwealth Games set, on which Gill Extra Bold appeared for the denominations. The floodgates seemed to open for Gill Sans from then onwards.

The setting up of Post Office Counters in 1986 gave rise to a rebranding exercise across thousands of locations. Initially a double-line sans serif (resembling Gill Sans Bold/Inline and made by B&M) was used for signage, but the look was revised in the early 1990s (fig.204). The cream-coloured, lozenge-shaped totem originally seen atop pillar boxes from the 1920s was redesigned with a red background and Gill Sans Medium for the legend 'POST OFFICE', and Gill Sans was also used on the fascias of many Post Office branches (p.10).

By the mid 1990s the majority of stamps and first-day covers featured Gill Sans somewhere, though this had reduced to a handful by the end of the decade. By the early 2000s the typeface was back in widespread use after a short rest. A 2004 set to commemorate the 250th anniversary of the Royal Society of Arts was a fine example of Gill Sans in use: not only did it feature in the denominations of all the designs, and with text on four of the set of five, but the entire typeface was the subject of the 57p stamp dedicated to Gill the designer (fig.205), the first stamp to celebrate a typeface.

By contrast, Gill Sans has featured on only a handful of coins. A £5 coin from 2010 was produced in advance of the London Olympic Games, while a set of four £5 silver coins was issued in 2015, all featuring quotes from Churchill set in Gill Sans Medium capitals. The Johnston typeface made its first appearance on stamps in a 'Classic Locomotives of England' miniature pack in 2011, and on a set of Olympic Games stamps in 2012, but it did not feature on any Royal Mint coins until the 150th anniversary of the London Underground in 2013 (fig.206). Meanwhile, even though the use of Gill Sans on postage stamps has decreased in recent years, it shows no signs of abating entirely: a first-day cover and miniature set of the 'Classic GPO Posters' for the Spring Stampex event in February 2016 featured Gill Sans and Max Gill's 1934 GPO logo.

205 (left)

To mark the opening of the Channel Tunnel in 1994, a set of stamps (designed by George Hardie and Jean-Paul Cousin) was issued by La Poste in France and the Royal Mail in the UK. All text was set in Gill Sans. Eric Gill is honoured in the Royal Society of Arts 250th anniversary commemoration set of 2004 (bottom). Gill Sans itself was the subject of the 57p stamp.

206 (above)

The first time that Johnston letters appeared on any Royal Mint coinage was in 2013 on two £2 coins (still in general circulation) commemorating the 150th anniversary of the Underground (top).

Although Kono had made an italic version of New Johnston, it had never really been used for signage. That changed in 2000 with the opening of the Croydon Tramlink system (fig.203), though signage reverted to New Johnston Medium in 2003. Bembo, which had been used by LT as a body font, was also scrapped at this time and TfL Johnston was used throughout to save licensing fees. The two PPP companies funding the Underground, Tube Lines and Metronet, both had their own logos, which used not Johnston or Arial but their own unnamed sans serifs.

'Transforming the Tube' – a massive rebuilding programme carried out during the 2000s – was all done in TfL Johnston and produced some memorable promotional material, although some of it was a little lazy as it relied on putting messages over roundels – something that would have horrified Frank Pick! From 2002 to the present, the multi-modal roundel masts in TfL Johnston lettering have been introduced outside stations in London. The contactless smart ticket for London, branded as Oyster Card, was launched in 2003, though oddly the decision was taken to use a non-Johnston sans serif for the logo (fig.207).

Johnston and Gill for the new millennium

Use of Gill Sans and ITC/P22 Johnston grew in the new millennium. In 2000, for example, the John Lewis Partnership ordered a bespoke Gills Sans for a rebrand of all stores. Designed by Sebastian Lester, and working with the Pentagram agency, specific letters were revised to give the face a modern look (fig.208). Two years later, arguably the largest Gill Sans letters in the world appeared on the side of the *Queen Mary* 2, launched in 2003 (fig.209). Meanwhile, Johnston was chosen for the way-finding system at the Westfield shopping centre at White City, London, in 2008. A revised Johnston Bold was adopted in 2011 by a small coffee shop in Hampshire called Mettricks. And a mixture of Johnston and Gill Sans were on display in the sets used by the American television drama *House* (2004–14).

Johnston escapes from London

In 2007, TfL's Overground branding was added to the former East London Line and its extensions at both ends. All stations were refitted with roundel signs in TfL Johnston, as were those of the Docklands Light Railway when it was rebranded as DLR the same year. TfL roundels featuring TfL Johnston were also introduced for

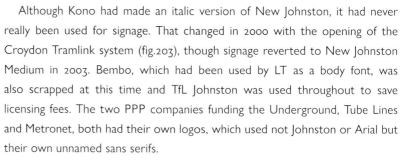

209

In the new millennium, Gill Sans and Johnston continued their use in popular culture and on icons like the *Queen Mary 2* (bottom left), launched in 2003. The Manic Street Preachers' 1994 sleeve for *The Holy Bible* featured Gill Sans Medium and a backwards 'R' (middle left; used again on *Futurology* in 2014). Whether this influenced the Church of England to begin using Gill Sans when Derek Birdsall revised the Common Worship Prayer Book in 2000 is not known (top). The Kaiser Chiefs have used Johnston for their CD covers – but also recently they've been using Gill Sans Bold for a logo (bottom right).

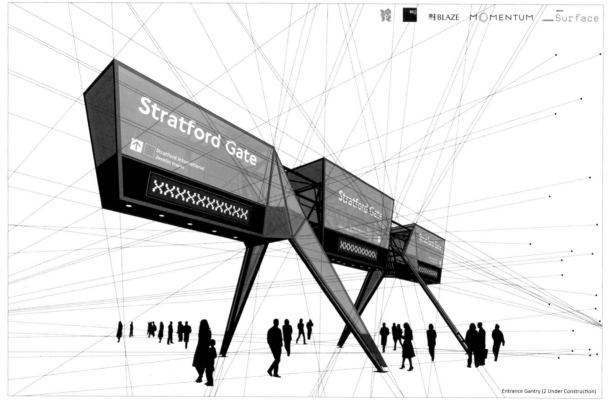

210

New Johnston was adopted for the way-finding element of the 2012 Olympics: a mock-up (centre) and actual photograph of the huge gantry sign at Stratford, London (top left). The first-time appearance of New Johnston outside the capital is shown at the Olympic venues of Weymouth (top right) and Windsor (top centre).

Integrating Legible London within station signing

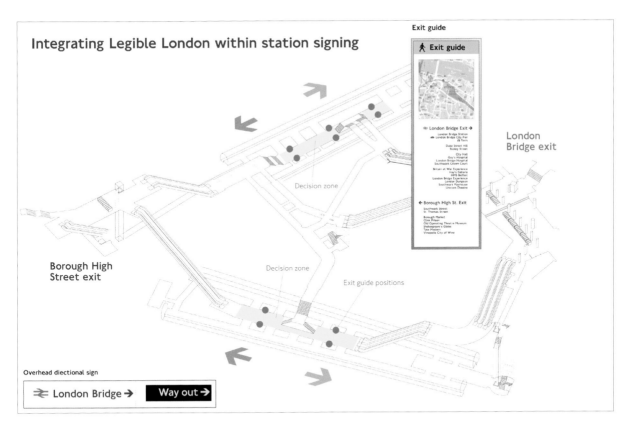

Exit guide

Exit guide

London Bridge exit

Decision zone

Decision zone

Exit guide positions

Borough High
Street exit

Overhead diectional sign

≷ London Bridge → | Way out →

211 (above)

In 2005, TfL began a study on how to make way-finding easier in the capital's streets. The process resulted in 'Legible London' pillars all set in New Johnston being erected for pedestrians at hundreds of locations in time for the London 2012 Olympics. District maps inside stations and at bus stops, as shown here, were upgraded to match the iconography.

212 (right)

The use of Johnston lettering on hundreds of new signs across the capital helped massively increase its presence in the public consciousness.

streets (fig.212), boats, cycle hire and taxis – effectively rolling out the typeface to all modes of transport across the capital, with the exception of the mainline and suburban railways.

Just as it had done 64 years before, London welcomed millions of spectators – not to mention all the athletes, officials and media – to the 2012 Olympic Games, for which managing their journey across the capital was seen as essential. Several design teams worked together on 'One Look' for a consistent graphic approach to every aspect of the Games. Michael Ives and Gareth Hague created the '2012 Headline' typeface, but for the way finding signs were exclusively in New Johnston. According to Geoff Holliday of GJandH consultancy: 'New Johnston featured across all way-finding in stations, transport networks, last mile approaches, inside the Olympic Park and venues across London and the UK.'[15] It was also the first time that TfL Johnston was officially sanctioned for use outside the capital (fig.211).

Gill Sans reborn

Customising typefaces is nothing new (*Grazia* magazine asked Monotype for a bespoke version of Gill Sans in 2010) but one of the most pleasing for Gill Sans was conducted by graphic designer Phil Baines when working on rebranding for the Ditchling Museum of Art + Craft. The museum had been extended and renovated and was due to re-open in 2013 with many of Johnston and Gill's artefacts and other work on display. Baines was commissioned to make a new sign for the entrance but customising letters was not part of his brief, as he explains:

> I was using Gill in wood type, and looking back at the Monotype catalogues I kept noticing minor differences in certain letters. The lower case 'a', 'b', 'd' and 'q', for example in 24pt case, all had variations [compared] to Monotype's. We thought that we could maybe do a custom version for Ditchling, so working with student Natalie Brown, I began digitising every letter, correcting 'a', 'b', 'd', 'p' and 'q', and looking at the spacing. When we'd come this far, we asked ourselves, 'Well, what if Gill had our tools?' and reproduced our changes so that it was consistent across light and bold weights too.[16]

The museum liked the result (fig.213), but facing the prospect of not securing a licence to alter the typeface, Baines contacted Rhatigan, then UK type director

DITCHLING MUSEUM OF ART+CRAFT

at Monotype, and was given special dispensation due to the importance of the museum for Gill.

Inspired by their work, Rhatigan examined the full range of Gill Sans created over its entire history, discovering more than 30 series in their books. Rhatigan's initial idea was to revisit some of those that had never been digitised, such as Cameo, Ruled and Shadow Line. A proposal to re-master the entire family gained momentum. A revision of Gill's seriffed typeface, Joanna, was included in the project too. Created in 1930–31 and named after one of his daughters, the face had been used by Gill for typesetting his *Essay in Typography*. Undertaken by George Ryan, type designer for Monotype, the work took over a year, but by November 2015 it was finished and the Gill Sans Nova range was launched in London, with 43 different varieties, several appearing for the first time (fig.214). Joanna Nova and Joanna Sans Nova (an entirely new face designed by Terrance Weinzierl) arrived at the same time, amounting to a total of 77 revised fonts – a truly significant achievement.

TfL Johnston revised

Information design specialist Doug Rose had studied spacing issues on bus blinds and in 2009 presented four new designs of Johnston to TfL.[17] In 2016, for its 'Transported by Design' initiative, TfL's Jon Hunter commissioned Monotype to revise TfL Johnston, briefing the company to reinstate some of the idiosyncrasies of the original, while keeping many of Kono's revisions. Designed by Marlou Verlome and Nadine Cahine and released in June 2016 as Johnston100, the typeface now included a 'hairline' weight, which added a beautiful new dimension, along with the '#' and '@' symbols (shown here for the first time in a book, figs 2 and 218). To celebrate the centenary, seminars were held and artworks were exhibited in London and at the Ditchling museum, spiritual home of Johnston and Gill.

A hundred years after the arrival of Johnston's Standard Alphabet, and 90 years since the appearance of Gill Sans, both typefaces are still going strong. Revised for the digital age, their continued future at the heart of British typography seems guaranteed. The Elizabeth line (fig.217), due to open fully in 2018, will feature Johnston100 lettering throughout. The BBC, John Lewis and the Church of England have no intention of replacing Gill Sans as their in-house typefaces. In the view of many commentators, this author included, Johnston and Gill have become the Helveticas of the UK, the faces of authority. In short, two very British types.

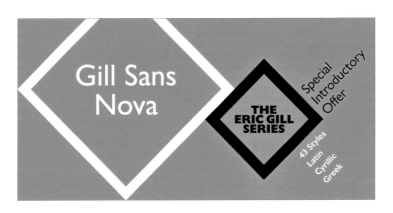

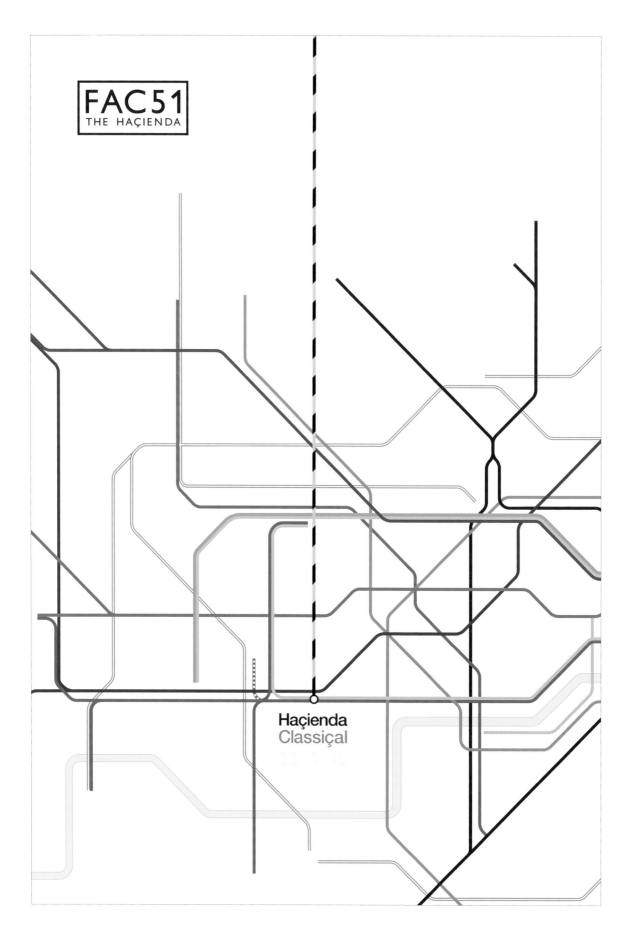

Epilogue

As Hermann Zapf once said of Johnston: 'Nobody had such a lasting effect on the revival of contemporary writing as Edward Johnston. He paved the way for all lettering artists of the twentieth century and ultimately they owe their success to him.'[1] Were it not for Johnston, Gill may not have embarked on lettering, focusing his energies more on sculpting and stone carving. But Gill took inspiration from his former teacher and carried it forwards. Without his contribution, the history of sans serifs in general, and of British typography in particular, might have turned out very differently.

As individuals, they were quite unalike. Some parts of their lives were lived at opposite ends of the moral compass, and while Gill was prepared to take on almost any job for a fee, Johnston was more discriminating, even if not as commercially astute: his total perfectionism would not allow him to deliver a piece of work that he was not fully happy with. Yet what both men had in common was a genius for typography – a finely attuned sense for devising not only what was needed for the project in hand but one that would endure.

Hundreds of sans serifs have been created since 1916, many typographers following in the footsteps of both Johnson and Gill, and new sans serifs will continue to be created. But the reslilence of both typefaces demonstrates how Johnston and Gill understood the quintessential shapes needed for block lettering. Formed to convey the utmost purity and clarity, each letter has, at the same time, a sense of individuality and a feeling of craftsmanship that echo the very earliest sans serifs. The reader is transported across two millennia, from Roman inscriptions on an ancient monument to a computer screen in the modern digital era. Johnston and Gill have contributed two of the simplest yet most graceful letterforms of the last century. For men of such dedicated religious conviction, they have created signs for all eternity.

219 (opposite)

A one-off poster created by Chestnut Studios to commemorate the Haçienda Classics event at the Royal Albert Hall in 2016. Epitomising the national significance of both typefaces, New Johnston is used for the date and Gill Sans features in the Haçienda logo, as it had been since the club's first opening in 1982 (p.156).

220 (above)

All the key figures mentioned in this book have been awarded blue plaques. Gill's is in Chichester, the other three in various parts of London. Erected in 1977, Edward Johnston's plaque in Hammersmith was set in the creator's own typeface, the first to be permitted this privilege. The same dispensation was allowed for two other plaques (not shown): Frank Pick's (1981) and Henry Beck's (2014).

Glossary of typographical terms

alternate
Different style or shape for the same **character** in a **typeface**.

apex
The point at which two **strokes** meet (usually at the top of a letter).

ascender
The **stroke** of a **lower-case** letter that rises above the **x-height**.

baseline
An invisible line on which most letters appear to sit.

black letter
Also known as Gothic script, black letter has the appearance of formal handwriting with a quill or pen. The form of the letter is relatively thick throughout, giving it an emboldened appearance, hence its name.

block letter/capital
Self-standing (as opposed to linked up, as in handwriting) individual letters, often used for teaching children to write. Typographically, another way of saying **sans serif**.

body copy/text
The main part of the text of a book, poster or article, excluding headings.

bold
A **weight** in which a letter has a thicker form than the standard **medium** version, making it appear darker.

bowl
The round part of a letter, such as 'P' or 'R', that contains a **counter**.

bracket
The joint between the main **stroke** and a **serif**.

cap height
Distance between the **baseline** and the top of the **upper-case** letters.

caster
A typecasting machine that creates individual letters by squeezing hot metal into (brass) moulds known as matrices. A composition caster was used for continuous **body text**, while the Monotype Super Caster (p.86) was mostly dedicated to casting type for one-off **display** headlines.

character
Any individual element of a **typeface**, from the letters and numbers to punctuation marks and other symbols.

cold typesetting
Where the letters are pressed directly on to the paper without the casting of hot metal (see **caster**).

condensed/extra condensed
The name given to a compressed or narrowed version of lettering within a larger **typeface** family. It allows more letters to be fitted into a line of text.

counter
The space entirely or partially enclosed within the bowl of a letter, such as a 'b', 'e' or 'o'.

crossbar
The horizontal **stroke** across the centre of an 'A' or 'H'.

cursive
Resembling handwritten or **italic** lettering.

descender
The **stroke** of a **lower-case** letter that projects below the **baseline**.

display
Text mostly designed for headlines or purely decorative used at a larger **point size**. Also referred to as 'titling'.

double crown
The standard poster size, 20 x 30 inches (50 x 76 cm). See also **double royal** and **quad royal**.

double royal
Poster size popular with the travel industry (particularly for advertising journeys by rail): 25 x 40 inches (63 x 101 cm). See also **double crown** and **quad royal**.

Egyptian
Another name for a **slab serif**. (See also p.14.)

extended

Also known as 'wide', a **letterform** within a larger **typeface** family that has been expanded horizontally but not vertically.

face

Short for **typeface**.

font

Also spelled 'fount', the physical or digital embodiment of a **typeface**.

foundary

A company or workplace where type is designed and/or produced.

glyph

The graphical representation of a character.

Grotesque/Grotesk

The German term for **sans serif**. (See also p.22.)

hairline

Both the thinnest part of a **stroke** and a term for the ultra-thin **weight** of a **typeface**.

hot-metal typecasting

See **caster**.

inline

A style of **typeface** that includes a light line scored on the inside of the **strokes** of a letter.

italic

Slanted **letterform** based on a sloping style of handwriting and often used for emphasis. More common in a **serif** than a **sans serif** family of type.

justify (text)

The adjustment of spacing between whole words and individual letters during typesetting so that the last letter of a line aligns with the end of the lines above and below it. (Sometimes achieved only by breaking a word at the end of a line and adding a hyphen.)

kerning

The adjustment of the space between individual letters so that it appears equal.

leading

The distance between lines of type, measured from **baseline** to baseline.

leg

The downward-slanted **stroke** on the letter 'k' and capital 'R'.

letterform

The overall shape of a letter; sometimes a synonym for **glyph**.

ligature

A **character** created by the joining together of two letters, e.g. 'æ' or 'œ'.

light

A style of **typeface** in which the **stroke** width is narrower than for the **medium** weight.

line block

A method of printing in which a reversed (negative) form of an image is transferred to a photosensitised metal plate. Exposure to light makes the emulsion acid-resistant so that non-exposed parts can be washed off. Ink sticks to the raised area, which can then be applied to paper for printing.

Linotype

A type-composing company whose machines were able to produce whole lines of words as single strips of metal.

lithograph

A printing process by which an image is applied as a waxy substance to the surface of a stone or metal plate and then covered in acid. The acid removes part of the surface, leaving the waxed area, which can then hold ink for transfer to paper.

lower case

Referring to the smaller letters (rather than the capitals or **upper case**) of a **typeface**. The term originates from the days when type was stored in large shallow drawers (cases) in a printing shop, the smaller letters being kept below the capitals.

masthead

Title of a magazine or journal given at the top of the front page, usually in **bold** or coloured **display** lettering.

medium

Also known as 'regular', the standard **weight** of a particular **typeface**.

monoline/mono-stroke

Letters in which the width of each **stroke** is roughly equal. They may be optically adjusted (lighter horizontal, for instance).

movable type

A method of printing that utilises movable parts to reproduce words and other elements of a printed document.

offset printing
A method of printing in which an image is covered in ink before being transferred first to a rubber roller or blanket and then to the printing surface.

outline
A style of **typeface** with a narrow line 'outlining' the edge of a **character**.

pantograph
A device, made up of hinged and jointed rods, for copying a drawing on a different scale.

petits-serifs
Barely discernable **serif** on a **stroke** that is otherwise **monoline**; usually added to a **sans serif** for decoration.

phototypesetting
Text generated by firing light through the negative of a letter onto photosensitive paper, usually at great speed.

pica
A unit of measurement for a **typeface**, about one-sixth of an inch in size or equivalent to 12 **points**. (See also p.20.)

point
Unit of measurement for a **typeface**, one point being equivalent to $1/72$ of an inch. (See also p.20.)

point size
The vertical measurement of lettering based on the **x-height**.

pull
A trial print-out of wooden or metal type in order to assess the accuracy of the letters set. Also known as a 'proof'.

punch cutter
A craftsperson who cuts letter punches in steel, from which copper matrices can be produced for type founding.

quad royal
A poster size of 40 x 50 inches (101 x 127 cm), the standard size for transport network maps. See also **double crown** and **double royal**.

regular
See **medium**.

roman
The most common upright (as opposed to **italic**) **typeface** style, often used to denote the **medium** (or regular) weight of a typeface.

sans serif
Letters that have no projecting features at the end of a **stroke**. See **serif**.

serif
Small line or projecting feature at the end of a **stroke**.

slab serif
A very thick, block-like **serif** with blunt or square **terminals**.

small cap
Capital letters that are shrunk to the same **x-height** as the **lower case** letters.

stem
The main vertical part of a **character**, e.g. the straight part of a 'b', 'l' or 't' in **upper** or **lower case**.

stroke
One or more lines, curved or straight, that make up a letter.

Super Caster (Monotype)
See **caster**.

tail
The **descender** of a 'q'.

terminal
The end of a **stroke**, the form either flat or curved depending on the style of **typeface**.

tick
Elongated **bracket** and **serif** added to numeral one to help distinguish it from other letters.

titling
See **display**.

tittle
The dot above an 'i' or 'j'.

typeface
A particular design of type, comprising the entire range of letters, numerals and punctuation. A typeface contains its entire family of individual fonts like medium, bold, italic etc.

upper case
The capital letters of a **typeface**, the term originating from the days of wooden and metal type when capitals were stored in the higher print drawer or case in a print shop.

weight
The relative darkness of a letter depending on the thickness of the **strokes**, defined as **bold**, **light**, **medium**, etc.

white space
The non-printed area within text or on a page.

x-height
A way of measuring a typeface based on the height of the **lower case** letter 'x' (i.e. excluding an **ascender** or **descender**).

Notes

Introduction

1 John Dreyfus, 'Mr Morison on Typographer', *Signature, New Series,* 3 March 1947, p.10

2 Steve Heller, *Wired* magazine blog, October 2015

Chapter 1

1 James Mosley's blog (http://typefoundry. blogspot.co.uk/2007/01/nymph-and-grot-update.html), first paragraph, 6 January 2007

2 James Mosley, *The Nymph and the Grot,* Friends of the St Bride Printing Library, London, 1999, p.17

3 Michael Twyman, http://faculty.education. illinois.edu/westbury/paradigm/twyman. html

4 James Mosley, op. cit. (*The Nymph and the Grot*), p.39

5 Robert Bringhurst, *The Elements of Typographic Style,* 2004

6 Author interview with Jeremy Tankard, January 2016

7 Justin Howes, *Johnston's Underground Type,* Capital Transport, Harrow Weald, 2000, p.31

8 Author interview with Jeremy Tankard, January 2016

9 Ian Mortimer and James Mosley, *Ornamented Types: Twenty-three Alphabets from the Foundry of Louis John Pouchée,* I. M. Imprimit, London, 1993

10 Author interview with Jeremy Tankard, January 2016

11 John Lewis, *Printed Ephemera,* Antique Collectors' Club, Woodbridge, 1962

12 Author interview with David Osbaldestein, February 2016

13 Catherine Dixon, 'Why We Need to Reclassify Type', *Eye Magazine,* vol.19, Winter 1995

14 James Mosley, op. cit., pp 11–12

Chapter 2

1 Priscilla Johnston, *Edward Johnston,* Barrie & Jenkins, 1959, p.49

2 ibid., p.66

3 ibid., p.67

4 ibid., p.68

5 ibid., p.87

6 ibid., p.96

7 Eric Gill, *Autobiography,* Jonathan Cape, London, 1940, p.98

8 ibid., p.119

9 Fiona MacCarthy, *Eric Gill,* Faber & Faber, London, 1989, p.41

10 Fiona MacCarthy, op. cit., p.71

11 Priscilla Johnston, op. cit., p.127

12 ibid., p.128

13 Priscilla Johnston, op. cit., p.149

14 ibid., p.150

15 Eric Gill, op. cit., p.136

Chapter 3

1 Author interview with David Lawrence (author of *Bright Underground Spaces: The Railway Stations of Charles Holden,* Capital Transport, Harrow Weald, 2008), February 2016

2 Doug Rose, *Tiles of the Unexpected,* Capital Transport, Harrow Weald, 2007

3 Douglas Rose in an interview with the author, Mark Ovenden, in *London Underground by Design,* Penguin, London, 2013, p.73

4 ibid., pp 84–7

5 David Bownes and Oliver Green, *London Transport Posters,* Lund Humphries, London, p.146

6 Christian Barman, 'Public Lettering', *Journal of the Royal Society of Arts,* vol.106, 1955, p.289

7 Christian Barman, *The Man Who Built London Transport: A Biography of Frank Pick,* David & Charles, Newton Abbott, 1979, p.43

8 ibid.

9 Priscilla Johnston, op. cit., p.199

10 Author interview with David Lawrence, February 2016

11 Justin Howes, op. cit., p.28, quoting an entry in Johnston's diary of 29 October 1915

12 Priscilla Johnston, op. cit., p.201

13 Justin Howes, op. cit., p.29

14 George S. Welch, *The Ship Painter's Handbook: With Useful Information for the General Painter and Decorator,* Gleves, Portsmouth, 1916, p.69

15 Justin Howes, op. cit., p.33

16 ibid., p.36

Chapter 4

1 Justin Howes, op. cit., p.47

2 Beverley Cole and Richard Durack, *Railway Posters 1923–1947,* Laurence King, London, 1992

3 Taylor, Richard, *Edward Johnston: A Signature for London,* Unicorn Publishing, London, 2016, p.40

4 Speaight, Robert, *The Life of Eric Gill,* P. J. Kenedy & Sons, New York, 1966, p.186

5 Fiona MacCarthy, op. cit., p.192

6 *Monotype Recorder,* vol.XLI, no.3, Autumn 1958, p.14, quoting from Gill's letter to Desmond Chute (1925)

7 *www.en.wikipedia.org/wiki/William_ Starling_Burgess*

Chapter 5

1 Christopher Skelton, *A Book of Alphabets for Douglas Cleverdon Drawn by Eric Gill*, September Press, Wellingborough, 1987, p.8, quoting from the original foreword by Douglas Cleverdon

2 Stated by Gill in a letter to Johnston of 1928: 'I hope you realise that I take every opportunity of proclaiming the fact that what the Monotype people call "Gill" sans owes all its goodness to your Underground letter'. Quoted in Priscilla Johnston, op. cit., p.204

3 *Monotype Recorder*, vol.XLI, no.3, Autumn 1958, p.15

4 James Mosley, http://typefoundry.blogspot.co.uk/2009/12/eric-gills-r-italian-connection.html

5 Quoted in https://www.myfonts.com/person/Frank_Hinman_Pierpont/

6 Author interview with Robert Nicholas, March 2016

7 Christopher Skelton, op. cit., p.10

8 *Monotype Recorder*, vol.XXXII, no.4, Winter 1933 (whole issue)

9 Curwen Sans type specimen, Curwen Press, London, 1928

10 Justin Howes, op. cit., p.73

11 Justin Howes, op. cit., p.52, quoting from letter to Johnston from A. L. Barber, September 1928

12 W. P. N. Edwards, *Visit of Lord Ashfield, Mr. Frank Pick and Mr. Charles Holden to Holland, Germany, Denmark and Sweden*, London Underground Group, April 1931

13 David Lawrence, *Bright Underground Spaces: The Railway Stations of Charles Holden*, Capital Transport, Harrow Weald, 2008, p.46

14 Eric Gill, *An Essay on Typography*, Sheed & Ward, London, 1931, p.27

15 ibid., p.48

16 ibid., p.49

17 Ben Archer, https://www.typotheque.com/articles/re-evaluation_of_gill_sans/, caption to an illustration

18 ibid., discussion of Granby

19 *Advertising Display Magazine*, October 1930, p.230

20 *LNER Magazine*, vol.23, no.1, January 1933, pp 3–5

Chapter 6

1 Ken Garland, *Mr Beck's Underground Map*, Capital Transport, Harrow Weald, 1994, pp 15–18

2 *Recorder*, vol.XXXII, no.4, Winter 1933, p.8

3 ibid., p.9

4 ibid.

5 Author interview with Sallie Morris, February 2016

6 Eric Gill, *Essay on Typography* (op. cit.), pp 48, 50, 51

7 Robert Harling in an article for *Penrose Annual*, vol.XXXIX, 1937, quoted in https://stoneletters.wordpress.com/2014/04/13/robert-harling-a-note/

8 Author interview with Sallie Morris, February 2016

9 Author interview with Dan Rhatigan, November 2015

10 Priscilla Johnston, op. cit., p.288

11 Nikolaus Pevsner, *Architectural Review*, August 1942

12 Priscilla Johnston, op.cit., p.305

Chapter 7

1 H. T. Carr and W. P. N. Edwards, *Report on the Standardization of Signs, Notices and Maps – Railways*, revised edn, London Passenger Transport Board, London, 1948

2 Author interview with Dan Rhatigan, October 2015

3 Author interview with Richard Oliver, March 2016

4 *Helvetica*, directed by Gary Hustwit, Plexi Film, 2007

5 Author interview with Robin Nicholas, March 2016

6 Author interview with John Kosh, March 2016

7 Author interview with David Kindersley, 2012

8 Email to author from Tim Demuth, 2013

Chapter 8

1 Walter Tracy's letter to Michael Levey, in the collection of Eiichi Kono

2 Jim Jansen's report on New Johnston, http://cargocollective.com/jimjansen/P22-Johnston-Typespecimen

3 Author interview with Eiichi Kono, February 2016

4 ibid.

5 ibid.

6 ibid.

7 Author interview with Tim Demuth, 2012

8 ibid.

9 Henrion Ludlow Schmidt, *Underground Railway Signing Study for London Transport*, May 1984

10 Author interview with Martin Lambie-Nairn, April 2016

11 BBC, *Credit and Branding Guidelines for BBC Television Programmes and for Radio Times*, 1998, p.2, quoting a memo from Colin Browne

12 http://www.newwriting.net/wp-content/uploads/2013/01/Skelton-Stephen-Gill-Sans.pdf, personal communication with Skelton.

13 Postal heritage website, http://www.postalheritage.org.uk/collections/getrecord/GB813_P_150_04_01)

14 Author interview with Mo Oshodi, January 2016

15 Author interview with Geoff Holliday, April 2016

16 Author interview with Phil Baines, March 2016

17 Email to author from Doug Rose, July 2016

Epilogue

1 Quoted in http://www.ejf.org.uk

Bibliography

Books and Papers

Baines, Phil, *Penguin by Design,* Allen Lane, London, 2005

——, and Catherine Dixon, *Signs: Lettering in the Environment*, Laurence King, London 2003

——, and Andrew Haslam, *Type and Typography*, Laurence King, London, 2002

Banks, Colin, *London's Handwriting: The Development of Edward Johnston's Underground Railway*, London Transport Museum, London, 1994

Barker, T. C., and Michael Robbins, *A History of London Transport*, 2 vols, Allen & Unwin, London, 1963, 1974

Barman, Christian, *The Man Who Built London Transport: A Biography of Frank Pick*, David & Charles, Newton Abbott, 1979

——, 'Public Lettering', *Journal of the Royal Society of Arts*, vol.106, 1955

Barr, John (ed.), *Stanley Morison: A Portrait*, Trustees of the British Museum, London, 1971

Bartram, Alan, *The English Lettering Tradition from 1700 to the Present Day*, Lund Humphries, London, 1989

——, *Street Name Lettering in the British Isles*, Watson-Guptill, New York, 1978

——, *Tombstone Lettering in the British Isles*, Watson-Guptill, New York, 1978

Berthold Wolpe: A Retrospective Survey, Victoria & Albert Museum with Faber & Faber, London, 1980

Blackwell, Lewis, *20th Century Type*, Laurence King, London, 2004

Bownes, David, and Oliver Green, *London Transport Posters*, Lund Humphries, London, 2008

Carr, H. T., and W. P. N. Edwards, *Report on the Standardization of Signs, Notices and Maps – Railways*, London Passenger Transport Board, London, 8 August 1938 (revised 1948, 1954, 1964)

Carter, Sebastian, *Twentieth Century Type Designers*, Lund Humphries, London, 1987

—— (ed.), 'Eric Gill: The Continuing Tradition', special issue of *Monotype Recorder*, new series, no.8, Autumn 1990

Child, Heather, *Formal Penmanship,* Lund Humphries, London, 1971

Clarke, Hedley, *Underground Bullseyes 1972– 2000*, Connor and Butler, Colchester, 2007

Clayton, Ewan, *Edward Johnston: Lettering and Life*, Ditchling Museum, Ditchling, 2007

Cole, Beverley. *It's Quicker By Rail: LNER Publicity and Posters 1923 to 1947*, Capital Transport, Harrow Weald, 2006

——, and Richard Durack, *Happy as a Sand Boy: Early Railway Posters*, HMSO, London, 1990

——, and Richard Durack, *Railway Posters 1923–1947*, Laurence King, London, 1992

Coles, Stephen, *The Geometry of Type*, Thames & Hudson, London, 2012

Cook, Brian, *Landscapes of Britain*, Batsford, London, 2010

Cousins, James, *British Rail Design*, Design Council, London, 1986

Cramsie, Patrick, *The Story of Graphic Design*, Harry N. Abrams, New York, 2010

Cribb, Ruth and Joe Cribb, *Eric Gill and Ditchling: The Workshop Tradition*, Ditchling Museum, Ditchling, 2007

Curwen, Harold, *Curwen Sans Type Specimen*, An Endless Supply, Birmingham, 2012

Daly, N, *The Demographic Imagination and the Nineteenth-Century City* Cambridge University Press, Cambridge, 2015

Dawson, Peter, *The Field Guide to Typography*, Thames & Hudson, London, 2013

Demuth, Tim, *The Anonymity of an In-house Designer*, GraficaMulti, Reading, 2011

Dixon, Catherine, 'Why We Need to Reclassify Type', *Eye Magazine*, vol.19, Winter 1995

Dobbin, Claire, *London Underground Maps: Art, Design and Cartography*, Lund Humphries, London, 2012

Dow, Andrew, *Telling the Passenger Where to Get Off*, Capital Transport, Harrow Weald, 2005

Edwards, W. P. N., *Visit of Lord Ashfield, Mr. Frank Pick and Mr. Charles Holden to Holland, Germany, Denmark and Sweden*, London Underground Group, London, April 1931

Evetts, L. C., *Roman Lettering: A Study of the Letters of the Inscription at the Base of the Trajan Column, with an Outline of the History of Lettering in Britain*, Pitman, London, 1938

Eye Magazine, Monotype Special Issue, vol.84, Autumn 2012

Font: Sumner Stone, *Calligraphy and Type Design in a Digital Age*, Edward Johnston Foundation and Ditchling Museum, Ditchling, 2000

Frutiger, Adrian, *Type, Sign, Symbol*, ABC Verlag, Zurich, 1980

Garfield, Simon, *Just My Type: A Book About Fonts*, Profile Books, London, 2010

Garland, Ken, *Mr Beck's Underground Map*, Capital Transport, Harrow Weald, 1994

Gill, Eric, *Art-Nonsense and other Essays*, Cassell & Co. and Francis Walterson, London, 1929
——, *Eric Gill: Autobiography*, Jonathan Cape, London, 1940
——, *An Essay on Typography*, Sheed & Ward, London, 1931
——, *Sculpture and the Living Model*, Sheed & Ward, London, 1932

Gill, Evan R., *The Inscriptional Work of Eric Gill*, Cassell & Co, London, 1964

Gray, Nicolete, *XIXth Century Ornamented Types and Title Pages*, Faber & Faber, London, 1951
——, *A History of Lettering*, Phaidon, London, 1986
——, *Lettering on Buildings*, Architectural Press, London, 1960
——, 'Slab-serif Type Design in England 1815–1845', *Journal of the Printing Historical Society*, vol.15, 1980/81

Green, Oliver, *Underground Art*, 2nd edn, Laurence King, London, 2001
——, and Jeremy Rawse-Davies, *Designed for London*, Laurence King, London, 1995
——, and Sheila Taylor, *The Moving Metropolis*, Laurence King, London, 2001

Handover, P. M., 'Black Serif', *Motif*, vol.12, 1964
——, 'Grotesque Letters', *Monotype Newsletter*, vol.69, 1963
——, 'Letters without Serifs' in *Motif*, vol.6, 1961

Harling, Robert, *The Letter Forms and Type Designs of Eric Gill*, Eva Svensson/ Westerham Press, Westerham, 1976

Henrion, Ludlow, Schmidt, *Underground Railway Signing Study for London Transport*, May 1984

Howes, Justin, *Johnston's Underground Type*, Capital Transport, Harrow Weald, 2000

Hutchinson, Harold, *London Transport Posters*, London Passenger Transport Board, London, 1963

Johnson, A. F., 'Fat Faces: Their History, Forms and Use', *Alphabet and Image*, vol.5, 1947
——, *Type Designs: Their History and Development*, Grafton, London, 1959

Johnston, Edward, and Eric Gill, *Manuscript & Inscription Letters for Schools & Classes & for the Use of Craftsmen*, John Hogg, London, 1909
——, *Writing & Illuminating & Lettering*, John Hogg, London, 1906

Johnston, Priscilla, *Edward Johnston*, Barrie & Jenkins, London, 1959

Lawrence, David, *Bright Underground Spaces: The Railway Stations of Charles Holden*, Capital Transport, Harrow Weald, 2008
——, *A Logo For London*, Capital Transport, Harrow Weald, 2000

Leboff, David, *The Underground Stations of Leslie Green*, Capital Transport, Harrow Weald, 2002

Levey, Michael F., *London Transport Posters*, Phaidon Press, London, 1976

Lewis, John, *Printed Ephemera*, Antique Collectors' Club, Woodbridge, 1962

Lloyd, Peter, *Vignelli Transit Maps*, RIT Cary Press, Rochester, NY, 2012

LNER Magazine, vol.23, no.1, January 1933

London Transport, *Tramlink Visual Identity Guidelines*, London, 1998
——, *Changing Stations*, LUL Architectural Services, London, 1993
——, *London Underground Sign Manual*, 1938, 1948, 1964, 2001
——, *Underground Railway Signing Study for London Transport*, London, 1984

MacCarthy, Fiona, *Eric Gill*, Faber & Faber, London, 1989

McLean, Ruari, 'An Examination of Egyptians', *Alphabet and Image*, vol.1, 1946

Middleton, Allan, *It's Quicker By Rail: The History of LNER Advertising*, Tempus, Stroud, 2002

Millington, Roy, *Stephenson Blake: The Last of the Old English Typefounders*, Oak Knoll Press, New Castle, DE, 2002

Monotype Recorder, vol.XXXII, no.4, Winter 1933

Morison, Stanley, *First Principles of Typography*, Macmillan, London, 1936
——, 'The Story of Gill Sans', *Monotype Recorder*, vol.XXXIV, no.4, Winter 1935–6

Mortimer, Ian, and James Mosley, *Ornamented Types: Twenty-three Alphabets from the Foundry of Louis John Pouchée*, I. M. Imprimit, London, 1993

Mosley, James, *The Nymph and the Grot*, Friends of the St Bride Printing Library, London, 1999
——, 'Trajan Revived', *Alphabet*, vol.1, 1964
——, 'The Type Foundry of Vincent Figgins, 1792–1836', *Motif*, vol.1, 1958

Müller, Lars, *Helvetica: Homage to a Typeface*, Lars Müller Publishers, Baden, 2005

Nesbitt, Alexander, *The History and Technique of Lettering*, Dover Publications, 1957

Ovenden, Mark, *London Underground by Design*, Penguin, London, 2013

——, *Transit Maps of the World*, Penguin, London, 2015

Parker, Mike, *Mapping the Roads: Building Modern Britain*, AA Publishing, Basingstoke, 2013

Rickards, Maurice, *The Public Notice*, David & Charles, Exeter, 1973

Roberts, Max, *Underground Maps After Beck*, Capital Transport, Harrow Weald, 2005

Rose, Douglas, *Tiles of the Unexpected*, Capital Transport, Harrow Weald, 2007

Schwandl, Robert, *Metros in Britain*, Robert Schwandl Verlag, Berlin, 2006

Shaw, Paul, *Helvetica and the New York City Subway System: The True (Maybe) Story*, Blue Pencil Editions, New York, 2009

Simon, Herbert, *Songs and Words: A History of the Curwen Press*, Allen & Unwin, London, 1973

Skelton, Christopher, *A Book of Alphabets for Douglas Cleverdon Drawn by Eric Gill*, September Press, Wellingborough, 1987

Speaight, Robert, *The Life of Eric Gill*, P. J. Kenedy & Sons, New York, 1966

Spencer, Herbert, *Pioneers of Modern Typography*, Lund Humphries, London, 1969

Spiekermann, Erik, and E. M. Ginger, *Stop Stealing Sheep and Find Out How Type Works*, Adobe, Berkeley, CA, 2003

Tracy, Walter, *Letters of Credit: A View of Type Design*, David R. Godine, Boston, MA, 2003

——, 'Why Egyptian?', *Printing History*, 31/32, 1994

Taylor, Richard, *Edward Johnston: A Signature for London*, Unicorn Publishing, London, 2016

Transport for London, *The London Games in Motion*, Laurence King, London 2013

Tschichold, Jan, 'Type Mixtures', *Typography*, vol.3, 1937

TwoPoints.net, *I Love Gill Sans*, Viction:ary, Hong Kong, 2012

Twyman, Michael, 'The Bold Idea: The Use of Bold-Looking Types in the Nineteenth Century', *Journal of the Printing Historical Society*, vol.22, 1993

——, *Printing 1770–1970*, Eyre & Spottiswoode, London, 1970

——, 'Typography Without Words', *Ultrabold*, vol.16, 2014

Updike, D. B., *Printing Types: Their History, Forms, and Use*, British Library Board, 1982

Welch, George S., *The Ship Painter's Handbook: With Useful Information for the General Painter and Decorator*, Gleves, Portsmouth, 1916

Wilbur, Peter, and Michael Burke, *Information Graphics: Innovative Solutions in Contemporary Design,* Thames & Hudson, London, 1998

Whitehouse, P. B., *Railway Relics and Regalia*, Country Life, London, 1975

Yorke, Malcolm, *Eric Gill: Man of Flesh and Spirit*, Constable, London, 1982

Webography

All About Lettering:
https://stoneletters.wordpress.com/2014/04/13/robert-harling-a-note/

Ben Archer on Gill Sans:
https://www.typotheque.com/articles/re-evaluation_of_gill_sans/

Edward Johnston Foundation:
http://www.ejf.org.uk/

Eric Gill Society:
http://www.ericgill.com/Harry Carter, *A Geometrical Approach to Letter Design: Renaissance and Modernism* (Washington University course):
http://courses.washington.edu/des376/sanserif.html

James Mosley's blog:
http://typefoundry.blogspot.co.uk/2007/01/nymph-and-grot-update.html

Jim Jansen's report on New Johnston:
http://cargocollective.com/jimjansen/P22-Johnston-Typespecimen

London Transport Museum:
Museum: http://www.ltmuseum.co.uk/
Photos and posters: http://www.ltmcollection.org/photos/

Michael Twyman on typographic cueing in the 1800s:
http://faculty.education.illinois.edu/westbury/paradigm/twyman.html

Monotype Imaging:
http://www.monotype.com

National Railway Museum:
http://www.nrm.org.uk/

Postal heritage site:
http://www.postalheritage.org.uk

Sebastian Carter on Frank Hinman Pierpont:
https://www.myfonts.com/person/Frank_Hinman_Pierpont/

UK road sign evolution:
http://www.cbrd.co.uk

Films

Helvetica, directed by Gary Hustwit, Plexi Film, 2007

House of Caslon, directed by Jonathan Martin (university project), 2013

Johnston and Gill Sans in use

Listed below are examples of the Johnston and Gill Sans typefaces in use, both past and present. This list is purely illustrative and could never be exhaustive (one-off book titles, albums and movies, for example, have not been included as they are far too numerous) but is intended to give a flavour of the sheer breadth and diversity in usage of these two typefaces since they first appeared. More examples can be found or submitted at the Twitter feeds #johnstoncentenary and #greatgillgathering.

Current or recent users
Be At One (cocktail bars), *Classic English Style* (online magazine), Fleet Operator Recognition Scheme, Galeries Lafayette,* Glass Animals (band), Happy Naturals,* Health Hub (Herne Hill), Isle of Wight Steam Railway,* Kaiser Chiefs (band), Lodge Café (Hyde Park), London Assembly, London 2012 Olympics,* Marina and the Diamonds (band),* MaxMara,* Mayor of London, Olympic Studios (Barnes),* Outpost Coffee (Nottingham), Ride with Pride (Routemaster bus), Routemaster destination blinds, Sawyer & Gray (restaurant), Southampton City Council (pavement walk), Southeastern trains, Spitfire mugs, Transport for London, UNiDAYS (website), Westfield (White City).

Former users
British Road Services, Empire Marketing Board, NorthMet.

GILL SANS

Current or recent users
SHOPS AND SERVICES, ETC
A.J. Wells (Newport), Amy Somerville, Asda Living, Autograph Fashion, Bamford & Sons, Barnardo's shops, Battle of Britain Monument (Victoria Embankment), BBC, Benetton, Bradford & Bingley Building Society, Bradford International Film Festival (20th), British Hospitality Association, Broadway Shopping Centre (Hammersmith), Brooklands Museum (Weybridge), Byron hamburgers, Castle Fine Art, Cavendish House (Hastings), Central Heating Services Ltd, City Chiropractic (Leeds), Collins Gem (books), Company of Cooks, Conran Shop, Considerate Constructors Scheme, FM Conway, Cotton Gardens (Kennington), Cousins Furniture,* Cunard (liners), Darwin Centre (Science Museum), Ditchling Museum of Art + Craft, Dwell, EasyJet,* English Heritage,* Evans Halshaw, Farnborough Leisure Centre, FlexiHerb, Flight Centre, Fish for Thought, Focalpoint Opticians,* Foyles (bookshop), Garlic Farm (Isle of Wight),* General

Motors,* Glastonbury Festival (2011), Greene King, Hare & Tortoise, Harrods Estates, Headmasters hairdressers, Health Elements, Healthy Living Centre (London), HM Treasury, H. Samuel (jeweller), Holland & Barrett,* Hope & Greenwood, Inmarsat, John Lewis, Kingfisher toothpaste, Language Link, Leon (restaurants), Livebait (restaurants), Lloyds Pharmacy, Loaf,* London Wetlands Centre, May2015.com (general election website), May Fair Hotel, Mettricks Tea & Coffee (Southampton), Moss Bros., Napier Watt,* National Railway Museum, Net-A-Porter, Newlec, Orchid (male cancer charity), Ordnance Survey,* Pearson Business School, Peyton and Byrne, Philips,* Post Office, Q Hotels Group, Quick hamburgers, Quilt Museum and Gallery (York), Rabbits Vehicle Hire (Reading), railway overbridges (London), Royal Botanic Gardens (Kew), Royal Exchange Theatre (Manchester), RSA Insurance Group, Save the Children, Shepherds Bush Housing Group, Sotheby's, St Brides Tavern (London), Stagecoach buses,* Snappy Snaps, Swan Shopping Centre (Leatherhead), Start Fitness, Swisse, Thursday Plantation, Tommy Hilfiger,* Twinings,* Ultra Chloraseptic, Vanilla Cupcake Kitchen, Victoria House (Bloomsbury Square), Volcano (Poole), Vulcan to the Sky Trust, Waitrose.

GOVERNMENT BODIES

Borough Councils: (London) Barnet, Bromley,* Islington, Haringey,* Greenwich, Southwark*; (other) Eastleigh, North Tyneside, Trafford. *City Councils*: Carlisle,* Gloucester, Leicester, Norwich, Plymouth, York. *County Councils*: Buckinghamshire, Cornwall, Cumbria, Lincolnshire, Norfolk,* Shropshire. *District Councils*: Barrow-in-Furness, Bracknell Forest, Burnley, Charnwood, Dover, Eastbourne, Forest of Dean, Great Yarmouth, Hart,* Mendip, Ryedale, South Cambridgeshire, Swale, West Lancashire,* Wychavon. *Police*: Cambridgeshire, Merseyside, Nottinghamshire, Police Scotland, Police UK, Scottish Police Authority, Thames Valley. *Other*: GOV.UK (website),* Government Procurement Service, Hampshire Superfast Broadband, Hantsweb, Royal Parks.*

Former users

Aerialite, Aldwych Theatre, Apple Newton, Atco lawnmowers,* Austin Reed,* Ballet Rambert, Birmingham City Transport, BOAC, British Motor Corporation,* British Railways, British United Air Ferries, British Waterways, Cadbury,* Carlton Television, *City Life* magazine, *City Limits* magazine, City of Birmingham Electricity Supply Department, Clacton-on-Sea tourist office, Derry & Toms Roof Garden, *Design for Today* magazine, Devon General buses, *Due South* magazine,* Elastoplast,* *Exercise One* (Joy Division fanzine), Faber & Faber, Glasgow Corporation, GMPTE (Greater Manchester Passenger Transport Executive),* Great Game of Britain, Hammersmith Borough Council, Hospital Plan Insurance Services, Imperial Airways, Jersey Government, Kendals,* Leicester City Transport, Liverpool Education Committee, Liverpool Transport, LMS (London, Midland & Scottish Railway), LNER (London & North Eastern Railway), London County Council, London Transport, Kelvin Scottish Omnibuses, Magnet Kitchens,* Manchester and Salford Equitable Co-operative Society, Manchester Corporation Transport Department, Marconigram, Marks & Spencer,* Marsh & Baxter, *Matador* magazine, Mavor & Coulson, Metrovick lamps, Midland Red buses,* Ministry of Agriculture, Ministry of Food, Ministry of Health, Ministry of Labour and National Service, Miss Selfridge,* National Health Service, National Savings, Network Rail,* North Eastern Electricity Board, Northern General Transport Company, Northern Rock Building Society, Our Price Records,* Penguin Books, *Poetry* magazine, Polytechnic Stadium/Quintin Hogg Memorial Ground (Chiswick), Port of Grimsby, Port of Immingham, Preston Corporation, Pye Records,* *Radio Times*, Rootes (Motors), Royal Air Force, Scottish Motor Traction, Scottish Veterans' Garden City Association, Scott's Porage Oats, Selfridges, Skytrain,* Skyways Hotel,* Southampton Ocean Terminal, Sunbeam motorcycles, Sunderland Corporation Transport, Thomas Nelson & Sons, Westminster Press, Women's Press (Canada), Woolworths.*

* The typeface has not been used by the company/institution for the main logo but on signage, etc.

Acknowledgements

This book would not have been possible without the help of:

Mike Ashworth, Phil Baines, Scott Bakal, Paul Barnes, Alex Bradshaw, Paul Brand, Simon Brooke, Cally, Margaret Calvert, Brogan Campbell, Nadine Chain, David Challis, Pat Chessell, Lucy Clark, Rob Clark, Matthew Clayton, Lis Clucks, David and Yvette Cohen, Beverley Cole, Emma Cole, Helen Conford, Jean Contois, Mark Coop, Alice Cowling, Steve Crowhurst, Rod Dale, Lucy Day, Peter Davies, Tim Demuth, Catherine Dixon, Keith Doyle, James Edwards, David Ellis, Phillip England, Dave Farey, Innes Ferguson, Gerald Fleuss, James Fooks-Bale, Isobel Frankish, Tom Furness, Simon Garfield, Nick Garrett, Simon GP Geoghegan, Rosie Gleeson, Jim Goldsmith, Marilyn Green, Garrett Haas, Pauline Hand, David Handsman, Amy Hawkins, Tim Hedley-Jones, Nathaniel Hepburn, Ben Hollebon, Geoff Holliday, Peter Hook, Anthony Howard, Jon Hunter, Mecca Ibrihim, Anna Ison, Eddie Jabbour, Jim Jansen, Simon Jenkins, Andrew and Angela Johnston, Lucy Jones, Sacha Kibley, Reka Komoli, Eiichi Kono, Kosh, Martin Lambie-Nairn, David Lawrence, Chris Leadbetter, David Leboff, Ian Leese, Seb Lester, Peter B. Lloyd, Edward Lord, Tom Lynch, Fiona MacCarthy, Jenny Manders, Anne Maningas, Philip Marriage, Chris Marshall, Darren Martin, Jonathan Martin, Angela Mason, Alistair Meek, Darren Meldrum, Marcello Minale, Stewart Montgomery, Nick Morgan, Sallie Jane Morris, Ian Mortimer, James Mosley, Sam Mullins, Simon Murphy, Paul Naylor, Robin Nicholas, Richard Oliver, David Osbaldestin, Mo Oshodi, Graeme Park, Richard Park, Kate Parker, Alan Pemberton, Jane Penston, Julian Pepinster, Robert Pool, Jean François Porchez, Rebecca Price, Gemma Rafferty, Kim Rennie, Dan Rhatigan, Bob Richardson, George Ritchie, Max Roberts, Matt Robertson, Simon Sadler, Nathan Savage, Peter Saville, Christopher Saynor, Carrie Scott, Sue Shaw, Susan Shearer, Rob Shepherd, Angela Silvestri, Andrew Simpson, Guy Slatcher, Julian Stockton, Jeremy Tankard, Richard Taylor, Mark Terry, John Thomason, Sarah Thorowgood, Alice Tonge, Stewart Tyson, Malou Verlomme, Caroline Walker, John Walters, Mike Walton, Richard B. Watson, Jim Whiting, Andy Williams, Mark Wolstenholme, YeOldBookworms, Yin and Yang, Gerry Ziegler and Pawel Zuchowski.

Image credits

Index